Vol. VI   No. 3

Home Study
Large-Print Edition

SUMMER QUARTER   June, July, August 2023

Editorial 2

Christ Proclaims the Kingdom

UNIT I: Understanding God's Kingdom

June   4—Upside-Down Kingdom—Matt. 5:1-16 4
June 11—A Perfect Kingdom—Matt. 5:17-18, 21-22, 27-28, 38-39, 43-44 9
June 18—A Victorious Kingdom—Mark 3:13-29; 6:6*b*-13 14
June 25—Growing God's Kingdom—Matt. 13:24-33 19

UNIT II: Responding to God's Kingdom

July   2—Praying to God—Luke 11:1-13 24
July   9—Accept God's Invitation!—Luke 14:7-11, 15-24 29
July 16—A Warning for the Hard-Hearted—Luke 16:19-31 34
July 23—Separating the Sheep and the Goats—Matt. 25:31-46 39
July 30—Ears to Hear—Matt. 13:9-17 43
Aug.   6—Forgiving One Another—Matt. 18:21-35 47

UNIT III: Entering God's Kingdom

Aug. 13—A Story of Forgiveness—Luke 15:11-24 51
Aug. 20—God's Gracious Rewards—Matt. 20:1-16 55
Aug. 27—God's Great Mercy—Luke 18:9-14 59
           Paragraphs on Places and People 63
           For Comfort and Challenge 64

Editor in Chief: Kenneth Sponsler

Edited and published quarterly by
THE INCORPORATED TRUSTEES OF THE GOSPEL WORKER SOCIETY
UNION GOSPEL PRESS DIVISION
Rev. W. B. Musselman, Founder
Price: $4.99 per quarter*
shipping and handling extra
ISBN 978-1-64495-324-2

This material is part of the "Christian Life Series," copyright © 2023 by Union Gospel Press. All rights reserved. No portion of this publication may be reproduced in any form or by any means without written permission from Union Gospel Press, except as permitted by United States copyright law. Edited and published quarterly by The Incorporated Trustees of the Gospel Worker Society, Union Gospel Press Division. Mailing address: P.O. Box 301055, Cleveland, Ohio 44130-0915. Phone: 216-749-2100. www.uniongospelpress.com

EDITORIAL

THE KINGDOM—NOW AND NOT YET

Kelly Hawver

God's kingdom was central to John the Baptist's and Jesus' teachings from the beginning of their ministries (Matt. 3:2; 4:17). They came to announce that God's kingdom was near. That caused quite a stir among the people of Israel. However, the religious leaders of Jesus' day were blinded by their own assumptions of what God's kingdom was to be and therefore rejected Jesus as the King they had been waiting for (12:14).

On one hand, the kingdom of God has always been the rule of a sovereign Monarch over all creation. On the other hand, the kingdom has yet to be fully consummated. Thus, the kingdom of God is a complicated subject.

Our first unit this quarter (lessons 1 through 4) lays a foundation for understanding the complexities of God's kingdom. It begins with the Sermon on the Mount. Jesus painted a vivid picture of the attitudes and actions that are expected from the citizens of God's kingdom (lesson 1). His description of the citizens of the kingdom shocked the first hearers as it shocks us today. God's kingdom is filled with people who would be rejected by the world's standards.

We will continue to examine Jesus' teaching from the Sermon on the Mount in lesson 2. In this portion of His sermon, Jesus revealed the heart of God in giving the law. God wants inward obedience. He wants us to obey the law out of an outflow of the attitude of our hearts.

In lesson 3, we will see how the disciples were being prepared for their mission. They walked with Jesus and learned about God's kingdom from Him; then He sent them out to spread the good news about it to surrounding villages. He endowed them with His Spirit so that they would have power behind the proclamation.

God's kingdom is the object of three parables in lesson 4. Through this series of stories, Jesus explained to His disciples (and us today) that the establishment of the physical reality of God's kingdom on earth began with His coming to live among us, but it also will not be completely manifested until a future date. In the meantime, evil will be in the world, and God has given us all we need to overcome it. As we wait for the full reality of God's kingdom, we must be faithful servants.

Unit II (lessons 5 through 10) concerns various responses to the message of God's kingdom. The model prayer Jesus posed to His disciples in lesson 5 shows how we work with God to further His kingdom. Because God has given this privilege to His children, He wants believers to depend on Him to meet their needs.

Two parables found in Luke's Gospel are the focus of lesson 6. These complementary illustrations were a sharp rebuke to assumptions the Jewish leaders made about who would be honored in

---

PLEASE NOTE: Fundamental, sound doctrine is the objective of The Incorporated Trustees of the Gospel Worker Society, Union Gospel Press Division. The writers are prayerfully selected for their Bible knowledge and yieldedness to the Spirit of Truth, each writing in his own style as enlightened by the Holy Spirit. At best we know in part only. "They received the word with all readiness of mind, and searched the scriptures daily, whether those things were so" (Acts 17:11).

God's kingdom. Only after recognizing and admitting one's spiritual poverty is one fit for God's kingdom.

In lesson 7, Jesus tells a parable that shows our response to the kingdom of God should include compassion and mercy for one's fellow man. It is the gospel that changes an individual and imparts a compassionate heart to those who know the Lord.

Lesson 8 relates to Christ's return and being prepared for that event. The righteous and the wicked have radically different futures. The first group is eternally blessed, while the second group is eternally condemned. Jesus will render the final judgment for all people.

Following the parable of the sower and the soils, Jesus explained the purpose of teaching by parables in lesson 9. Parables gave the followers of Jesus who were desiring to know more a window into the mysteries of God's kingdom so that they would have more understanding. At the same time, those who were not following Him were left in the dark.

The final lesson in the unit covers a story Jesus told in answer to Peter's question about forgiveness. We will learn how our response to an offense should reflect what we have received from God. The story teaches that we should graciously and endlessly forgive others, just as God has forgiven us. A spirit of forgiveness should be unlimited, and we should never tally the number of times we extend mercy.

The last unit (lessons 11 through 13) centers on how one enters God's kingdom, that is, salvation. In lesson 11, the best known of all Jesus' parables, the parable of the lost son, stresses how graciously God forgives and welcomes those who repent and turn to Him in faith and how all heaven rejoices when this occurs.

Lesson 12 expounds on God's goodness to those who come into His kingdom. God deals with people as He wills, not as people sense fairness. His mercy and grace are extended to all people because of their need. No matter what point in life a person trusts Jesus as Saviour, we should be overjoyed for them receiving God's gracious gift of salvation.

The story in lesson 13 reveals that God is sovereign in the matter of eternal rewards and does not judge as man does. The familiar story of the tax collector and the Pharisee makes it clear that there is no place for boasting before God. Indeed, those we might consider last may be honored most highly by God. Only those who are humble enough to admit their sin and simply trust the Lord will enter His kingdom.

This quarter's study shows us that when we are living in anticipation of Christ's return and the ultimate manifestation of God's kingdom, we will be diligently proclaiming His message, seeking the lost, and rejoicing over their salvation. We will also practice forgiveness toward one another as we strive to live compassionate, selfless lives.

Home Study

Scripture Lesson Text

MATT. 5:1 And seeing the multitudes, he went up into a mountain: and when he was set, his disciples came unto him:

2 And he opened his mouth, and taught them, saying,

3 Blessed are the poor in spirit: for theirs is the kingdom of heaven.

4 Blessed are they that mourn: for they shall be comforted.

5 Blessed are the meek: for they shall inherit the earth.

6 Blessed are they which do hunger and thirst after righteousness: for they shall be filled.

7 Blessed are the merciful: for they shall obtain mercy.

8 Blessed are the pure in heart: for they shall see God.

9 Blessed are the peacemakers: for they shall be called the children of God.

10 Blessed are they which are persecuted for righteousness' sake: for theirs is the kingdom of heaven.

11 Blessed are ye, when *men* shall revile you, and persecute *you,* and shall say all manner of evil against you falsely, for my sake.

12 Rejoice, and be exceeding glad: for great *is* your reward in heaven: for so persecuted they the prophets which were before you.

13 Ye are the salt of the earth: but if the salt have lost his savour, wherewith shall it be salted? it is thenceforth good for nothing, but to be cast out, and to be trodden under foot of men.

14 Ye are the light of the world. A city that is set on an hill cannot be hid.

15 Neither do men light a candle, and put it under a bushel, but on a candlestick; and it giveth light unto all that are in the house.

16 Let your light so shine before men, that they may see your good works, and glorify your Father which is in heaven.

NOTES

Upside-Down Kingdom

Lesson Text: Matthew 5:1-16

Related Scriptures: Psalm 24:1-6; Isaiah 66:1-2;
Luke 6:20-26; Hebrews 11:36-38

TIME: A.D. 28   PLACE: mountain near Capernaum

GOLDEN TEXT—"Blessed are they which do hunger and thirst after righteousness: for they shall be filled" (Matthew 5:6).

Lesson Exposition

The Saviour announced that the kingdom of God was drawing near (Matt. 4:17). What attitudes and actions were appropriate for a citizen of God's kingdom? Christ answered this question in what is known as the Sermon on the Mount (chaps. 5—7). Although Jesus' primary audience would have been His disciples, there was a larger crowd of people who listened to Him teach (7:28).

THE SERMON'S SETTING—
Matt. 5:1-2

The "multitudes" (vs. 1) who came to hear Jesus' sermon are presumably the same as the "great multitudes" of 4:25 who followed Him. Some of them came from regions nearly a hundred miles away to listen to Jesus teach. God's supreme Old Testament revelation—the law—was given by Moses, accompanied by thunder and lightning, from Mount Sinai. One greater than Moses gave this sermon from a mountain region presumed to be near the Sea of Galilee.

As the master Teacher, Jesus employed the normal sitting posture of a Jewish rabbi. The ethics that He taught in His sermon contrasted sharply with the legalism of His religious opponents, who were absorbed with external righteousness. Jesus launched His Sermon on the Mount by overthrowing such an approach to life.

THE SERMON'S BLESSINGS—
Matt. 5:3-12

For the poor in spirit (Matt. 5:3). In this verse, we are immediately struck by the presence of the word "blessed." This refers to the spiritual wellness of believers. The term conveys the idea of being the privileged recipient of God's favor and thus enjoying a happier end than the wicked. Jesus' various declarations of blessedness in this sermon are commonly called the Beatitudes.

Jesus pronounced His first blessing on the "poor in spirit," which is a reference to humility. These are believers who have been stripped of their own securities and thus feel deeply their need for God. The Saviour's redemption, not their own goodness, is the basis for their citizenship in heaven.

For the mournful (Matt. 5:4). Jesus pronounced His second blessing on the mournful, who will receive God's comfort. Those who mourn do so because they know they have transgressed against the Lord, and they cry in confession and repentance, which is a reflection of their humble spirit.

These believers do not look to the world for satisfaction, joy, or comfort; rather, they find these things in the Saviour alone. When they come to Jesus in humility and faith, confessing their sins, He enters their lives and stays there with the sweet assurance of His forgiveness.

For the meek (Matt. 5:5). Jesus gave His third blessing to the meek and promised them the earth as an inheritance. Meekness has two aspects. On the one hand, the meek bear up under provocations, control their feelings, and refuse to get even. On the other hand, they are courageous, generous, and courteous. They put others, not themselves, first.

Here we find Jesus explaining the values of the kingdom. Relationships, possessions, information, prayer, money, and power are a few of the categories He redefined from God's perspective. Jesus showed that following Him involves radical change. For most of us, this means undoing the way we have always acted and reconsidering traditional sources of wisdom from our family, friends, and culture. To become like Jesus requires us to do a tough-minded review of our moral values and lifelong goals and dreams.

For the spiritually hungry (Matt. 5:6). Jesus next blessed those who long for righteousness and promised to fulfill their desires. The attitude is one of desiring God above all things and seeking to be in a right relationship with Him and others. While greed, injustice, and violence consume the unsaved, believers yearn for justice and goodness to be established.

In these first four beatitudes, there is a logical progression. First, we admit our spiritual bankruptcy (vs. 3). Seeing ourselves as "poor in spirit" causes us to "mourn" (vs. 4) our condition. Because we grieve over our sorrowful state, we come to a correct notion of ourselves, which makes us humble and meek (vs. 5). After accepting the appraisal arrived at in verses 3-5, we are ready to "hunger and thirst after righteousness" (vs. 6).

For the merciful (Matt. 5:7). Jesus then blessed the merciful and said they will be treated with mercy. This verse is talking about having a gracious disposition toward others. The merciful are kind, charitable, and ready to sympathize with the sufferings of the afflicted. They long for justice but are not harsh and cruel, and they seek to be generous to all by showing the love of God without partiality or preconditions.

For the pure in heart (Matt. 5:8). Jesus gave His sixth blessing to the pure in heart and promised that they will see God. The focus here is on being genuine and honest in all one's dealings. Such purity requires spiritual discipline and self-control. It renounces self-love for the love of God.

Sin is the enemy of moral purity, and popular ideas and activities conspire to undo it. The world ridicules and taunts the virtuous for not having fun, but instead of fun, the pure receive the greatest gift of all, namely, a personal encounter with the living God. When we come to know Him through faith in Christ, we are truly fulfilled.

For the peacemakers (Matt. 5:9). In the seventh beatitude, Jesus pronounced a blessing on "the peacemakers." In saying they will be called "children of God," Jesus meant they will become spiritual members of God's heavenly family (cf. John 1:12; Eph. 1:5). Peacemakers do not merely stay cool, calm, and collected but also work for peace in their families, schools, churches, businesses, and communities.

Jesus is the ultimate peacemaker, for He destroyed the enmity between sinners and God (II Cor. 5:18-19; Eph. 2:13-18). Jesus not only brings us peace with God but also heals our broken relationships.

For the persecuted (Matt. 5:10-12). In the final beatitudes, Jesus blessed the persecuted and promised them the kingdom of heaven. He taught that when Christians stand up for truth, righteousness, and goodness, they will be slandered and insulted. Such persecution arises when believers take a stand for righteousness and are known as followers of Christ.

Jesus gave two reasons His harassed followers should accept their circumstances with an attitude of joy. First, they ought to realize that their eternal reward will exceed their wildest expectations. Second, they can remember that God's enemies also mistreated His prophets.

As followers of Christ, we should not be shocked when we are slandered, physically harmed, or targeted for malicious rumors. Although we feel the intense pain of such injustices, we can persevere by holding on to the promise of God's richest blessings.

For instance, Jesus said that heaven belongs to the persecuted. By this He meant they will have a place of distinction in the kingdom of God. In this present world, many believers are harassed and abused by others for the cause of Christ. The world might regard them as nobodies, but God considers them people of honor who should be given nothing less than unending joy in His presence.

THE SERMON'S CHALLENGES—Matt. 5:13-16

To be salt (Matt. 5:13). Jesus noted that when salt becomes contaminated with foreign substances, it can lose its distinctive flavor and preservative qualities. When this happens, people will discard the worthless mineral. Jesus was figuratively referring to the spiritual qualities that should be present in His disciples; in other words, they need to have a wholesomeness about them that enables them to be a blessing and a moral preservative in the world.

To be light (Matt. 5:14-16). Jesus declared that His followers, as the light of the world, are to be a reflection of God's love. Also, they are to radiate the knowledge and presence of God to people living in spiritual darkness or ignorance.

Given these statements, it is not surprising that Jesus told His disciples to let their light shine before others. He wanted the unsaved to see the good works that God's grace produces in the lives of believers. As a result, the lost may be drawn to God's saving power and give Him glory.

—*Dan Lioy.*

PRACTICAL POINTS

1. Jesus is willing to encounter us wherever we are with the truth of His Word (Matt. 5:1-2).
2. The genuine recognition of our spiritual poverty and sadness is the starting point for renewal and growth in the Lord (vss. 3-4).
3. God is well pleased with such virtues as meekness, mercy, and purity of heart (vss. 5-8).
4. Our active promotion of peace at home and abroad meets with the Lord's approval (vs. 9).
5. When others harass us for our faith, God manifests His grace and glory upon us (vss. 10-12).
6. Instead of spiritually compromising, we should be a morally preserving influence in the world (vs. 13).
7. Through the grace of God, we can shine the light of His truth among the lost (vss. 14-16).

—*Dan Lioy.*

FOR DAILY MEDITATION

MONDAY, May 29.   II Cor. 7:8-13.
Comforted by repentance. Addressing sinful behavior among God's people can initially cause discomfort. Doing so, however, eventually resulted in comfort and great joy for the apostle Paul. His severe, yet loving words of exhortation to the Christians in Corinth helped in bringing about repentance in their lives. God's desire is to produce godliness in and through us.

TUESDAY, May 30.   Isa. 66:1-2.
Humility draws God's attention. Can you actually do anything *for* God? He is our all-powerful Creator and Sustainer. His majesty is demonstrated by, but cannot be contained within, all of heaven and earth. And yet He is mindful of us and delights when we recognize and acknowledge our lowliness in comparison to the infinite heights of His greatness. He blesses those who humbly trust and follow His guidance. There is great joy in following the One who created and loves us.

WEDNESDAY, May 31.   Rev. 21:1-4.
New heaven and new earth. The devastating effects of sin and the separation from God that it brings can be detected throughout creation and all of life's experiences. Pain and suffering are inevitable because of sin. But through faith in Jesus Christ, believers are restored to a right relationship with God and will live with Him forever. How encouraged are you to know that there is no pain or problem that will not have been wiped away as you live in God's glorious presence?

THURSDAY, June 1.   Heb. 11:36-38.
Suffering prophets. While living a life filled with leisure, luxury, and comfort might seem appealing, just the opposite was often the reality for many of those who faithfully trusted the Lord while boldly proclaiming the truth of His Word. Severe persecution is still a present reality for missionaries and other Christians throughout the world. By continuing to look to the Lord, God's people can find strength to endure. We can never face any challenge alone because our God and Saviour is with us.

FRIDAY, June 2.   Ps. 24: 1-6.
Who receives God's blessing? Students can make exhibits of the solar system in which miniature models of planets hang from thin pieces of string or wire. They might even include such things as stars and comets. But God hung the entire universe on nothing but His own power and might. All of creation belongs to Him. Blessed is the person who remains true in worship of our almighty Creator—the Lord God.

SATURDAY, June 3.   Luke 6:20-26.
The Beatitudes. Happiness is a highly sought-after commodity. The problem for those of the world is that they try to obtain it apart from God. A true sense of happiness and satisfaction comes from trusting the Lord and being content with His provisions for your situations. All the pleasures of this world are short-lived, but the joy given by the Lord sustains His people and lasts forever.

SUNDAY, June 4.   Matt. 5:1-16.
Who are kingdom citizens? There can be more to an optical illusion than initially meets the eye. In a similar way, those who appear to be rejected by God, according to the world's standards, are in fact blessed beyond measure when their faith is in the Lord. By recognizing your spiritual poverty, you can become rich in faith. And your faith in Jesus brings you into God's kingdom as a beloved citizen.

—Reginald Coats.

LESSON 2   JUNE 11, 2023

SCRIPTURE LESSON TEXT

MATT. 5:17 Think not that I am come to destroy the law, or the prophets: I am not come to destroy, but to fulfil.

18 For verily I say unto you, Till heaven and earth pass, one jot or one tittle shall in no wise pass from the law, till all be fulfilled.

21 Ye have heard that it was said by them of old time, Thou shalt not kill; and whosoever shall kill shall be in danger of the judgment:

22 But I say unto you, That whosoever is angry with his brother without a cause shall be in danger of the judgment: and whosoever shall say to his brother, Raca, shall be in danger of the council: but whosoever shall say, Thou fool, shall be in danger of hell fire.

27 Ye have heard that it was said by them of old time, Thou shalt not commit adultery:

28 But I say unto you, That whosoever looketh on a woman to lust after her hath committed adultery with her already in his heart.

38 Ye have heard that it hath been said, An eye for an eye, and a tooth for a tooth:

39 But I say unto you, That ye resist not evil: but whosoever shall smite thee on thy right cheek, turn to him the other also.

43 Ye have heard that it hath been said, Thou shalt love thy neighbour, and hate thine enemy.

44 But I say unto you, Love your enemies, bless them that curse you, do good to them that hate you, and pray for them which despitefully use you, and persecute you.

NOTES

A Perfect Kingdom

Lesson Text: Matthew 5:17-18, 21-22, 27-28, 38-39, 43-44

Related Scriptures: Acts 14:8-18; Romans 9:30—10:4;
I Corinthians 3:11-15; James 2:10-13

TIME: A.D. 28   PLACE: mountain near Capernaum

GOLDEN TEXT—"Think not that I am come to destroy the law, or the prophets: I am not come to destroy, but to fulfil" (Matthew 5:17).

Lesson Exposition

Do you keep a mental checklist of the things you do that broadcasts to those who are watching that you are a Christian? Maybe instead it is a list of guiding principles that keeps you from doing the "wrong" thing. Or it could be a regimen of daily spiritual tasks that you squeeze in between eating your breakfast and brushing your teeth. It is tempting to believe that adhering to these self-imposed rules is all it takes to please God. And you would not be alone. We all are prone to do this. In fact, it was what religious leaders in Jesus' time often did.

Jesus was not a Pharisee and did not think highly of their interpretations of the law and the additional traditions they imposed on God's people (Matt. 23:23). While the Pharisees may have had good intentions of protecting people from getting anywhere close to breaking God's law, the end result of their additional rules was that these "guardrails" became more important to them than the actual law. When Jesus would not conform to these additional rules, He was accused of being a lawbreaker.

This week's lesson text continues our look at Christ's Sermon on the Mount (Matt. 5—7). In these passages, Jesus taught the real meaning of the law, which He came to fulfill. He explained that the law was fulfilled by the righteous intent of the heart and not just by the outward act. The writer of Proverbs tells us, "As [a man] thinketh in his heart, so is he" (23:7). This was a new approach that was in contrast to pharisaic teachings.

Later Paul would come to explain that the law is unable to make us righteous but instead acts as a mirror showing us our inability to be righteous (cf. Rom. 8:1-8). Not leaving us to languish in this hopeless inability to meet God's standards, Jesus came to meet the requirements of righteousness in our place.

CHRIST AND THE SCRIPTURES—Matt. 5:17-18

The fulfillment of the Scriptures (Matt. 5:17). Jesus made it clear that He had come not to abolish the Law or the Prophets but to fulfill them. The terms "the law" and "the prophets" together refer to the entire Old Testament (cf. Acts 13:15).

Christ is the fulfillment of the Law and the Prophets in His Person, words, and works (28:23). In a post-resurrection appearance to two of His disciples, "beginning at Moses and all the prophets, [Christ} expounded unto them in all the scriptures the things concerning himself" (Luke 24:27).

The authority of the Scriptures (Matt. 5:18). Jesus solemnly declared that fulfillment extended to the smallest letter and stroke of a letter in the Hebrew text. The smallest Hebrew letter is the "jot," which resembles an apostrophe. The "tittle" is the stroke of the pen that distinguishes several pairs of similar Hebrew letters from each other. Jesus upheld the full authority of the Old Testament Scriptures down to the smallest part of the letter.

Christ affirmed that heaven and earth will not pass away until the Scriptures are fulfilled down to the very letters of the text.

CHRIST AND THE PHARISAIC TRADITIONS—
Matt. 5:21-22, 27-28, 38-39, 43-44

Jesus rejected the Pharisaic traditions with His "Ye have heard that it was said . . . but I say unto you" contrasts. The Pharisees taught that righteousness consisted in meticulous outward conformity to the Mosaic Law, but Jesus taught that the true intent of the law went far deeper than mere outward conformity to a code.

By the authority given to Him by His Father, Jesus dealt with the matters of the heart by taking God's laws to a new level. He declared that only those whose righteousness exceeded that of the Pharisees would enter His kingdom (vs. 20). This kind of righteousness had to be more than just an outward appearance, but one that was from a heart that desired to please God above man.

As we examine our own hearts and motivations for serving the Lord, ask the Holy Spirit to reveal to you when your motivations do not come out of a holy desire but a selfish one.

Murder (Matt. 5:21-22). The Pharisees correctly taught that murder is wrong and punishable by death (Ex. 20:13; 21:12-17; 22:18-20), but they did not address the attitudes that lead to murder. Jesus did not deny that homicide is a sin, of course, but He made it clear that the prohibition against murder extends to the underlying attitude.

Jesus taught that anyone who was angry with his brother and demeaned him without a cause was subject to legal judgment by the local authorities.

The term "Raca" (Matt. 5:22) means "empty-head." It was used to show contempt for others who were considered worthless. The court, or council, was the Jewish court (Deut. 16:18), also called the Sanhedrin, or the highest court, which was called the Great Sanhedrin.

Even worse was to call someone a fool. To do so was the equivalent of labeling that person as someone who did not believe in God. "The fool hath said in his heart, There is no God" (Ps. 14:1).

The severest judgment was "hell fire" (Matt. 5:22). The word translated "hell" is from the Greek word for "Gehenna." Gehenna was the place in the Valley of Hinnom outside Jerusalem where garbage and the corpses of criminals were dumped and burned. It came to symbolize the place of eternal punishment for the wicked (10:28).

In our day, we may have moved beyond anger to a state of rage that can rarely be justified. Our pride and self-centeredness are exposed by how easily we fly off into a tantrum. Also, since social media seems to add fuel to this flame of rage, do we examine our contributions to these conversations in light of the way Christ has asked us to?

Adultery (Matt. 5:27-28). The Pharisees' teaching focused on the outward act of illicit sexual union (Ex. 20:14). Jesus taught that adultery begins with the lust of the heart, which leads to the physical act. This is more than a casual glance at a beautiful person. This is a continual stare that creates an internal desire. The lustful desire is wrong and also must be avoided because lust, even apart from the act, is also adultery.

Retaliation (Matt. 5:38-39). The Pharisees taught that it was always right to follow the law of retaliation (Ex. 21:23-25; Lev. 24:20; Deut. 19:21). This law provided boundaries to make sure that the punishment fit the crime and did not exceed the offense (Deut. 19:4-7).

Jesus taught that while the offended had their rights, they did not necessarily have to claim them. When wronged by being struck on the cheek, they did not have to strike back; instead, they were to act in grace, humility, and selflessness. Christ set the example when He was so severely mistreated (I Pet. 2:23). Paul exhorted Christians not to avenge ourselves but to let God take care of it, while we "overcome evil with good" (Rom. 12:19-21).

Hatred of enemies (Matt. 5:43-44). The Pharisees taught that one should love his neighbor and hate his enemies. To hate one's enemies was another man-made tradition that went beyond the law.

In Luke's Gospel, Jesus illustrated this very point to the man who asked how to define who his neighbor was (10:25-37). At the end of the story, the man rightly answered that the neighbor was the one who "shewed mercy" on the injured man (vs. 37).

Jesus taught that a person should show compassionate love even for his enemies. This included returning blessing for cursing, good deeds for hatred, and prayer for persecution.

This extension of love is indicative of a vital relationship with God the Father (Matt. 5:45). He loves sinners upon whom He causes the sun to rise and sends the rain for their crops. True righteousness is in harmony with the character and heart of God.

—*Jack Riggs.*

PRACTICAL POINTS

1. Christians can have complete confidence in the Scriptures just as Jesus Himself did (Matt. 5:17).
2. God's Word is always true and will find complete fulfillment without any exceptions over time (vs. 18).
3. Believers should always treat other people with respect regardless of who they might be (vss. 21-22).
4. We must guard our hearts from lustful thoughts, which are contrary to God's character and righteousness (vss. 27-28).
5. God desires that believers show humility and grace to others when offended by them (vss. 38-39).
6. Godliness is expressed by showing compassion and mercy to those who hate and despise us (vss. 43-44).

—*Jack Riggs.*

FOR DAILY MEDITATION

MONDAY, June 5.   Rom. 9:30—10:4.

Unbelieving Israel. Being religious does not equate with being right with God. As zealous as many of the people of Israel were, they failed to trust Jesus as Messiah and Saviour. God's forgiveness and salvation are readily available to all who put their faith in Jesus Christ and what He accomplished with His death and resurrection. How might you help someone struggling to understand that God saves those who trust His Son, Jesus, for the glory of His own grace?

TUESDAY, June 6.   I Cor. 3:11-15.

Building on the foundation of Christ. Without a strong foundation, a building is doomed to collapse quickly. Christ and His finished work at the cross is the foundation upon which our faith and salvation is forever established. Our intentions and motives in ministry should be driven by our love for Him. Those who serve the Lord with pure hearts will even be rewarded for what *He* accomplishes through their lives.

WEDNESDAY, June 7.   Jas. 2:10-13.

Mercy over judgment. God's just wrath against sin was withheld from us because of His great mercy. No one is without sin, and no one deserves His deliverance. But that did not prevent Jesus from giving His life for us so that God's mercy could justly be extended to us. As a recipient of God's mercy, you are called by Him to show mercy to others.

THURSDAY, June 8.   Acts 14:8-18.

Common grace. Some of the letters and numbers on an eye chart can be difficult to read from where you are standing. God ensures, however, that His grace and goodness can be seen from anywhere in the world. His undeserved favor is bestowed upon His people and those who oppose Him. When opportunities arise, we should follow the example of Paul and Barnabas and help people to understand that only the Lord is to be worshipped.

FRIDAY, June 9.   Ps. 5:4-8.

God hates evil. Everything that is sinful and evil is in opposition to God and His holiness. He does not *decide* to hate sin any more than a fire decides to consume paper. God's nature simply does not permit sin to be in His presence. Because of His unfailing love for us, He has always made provisions for people to have fellowship with Him. The perfect provision that enables us to enjoy fellowship with Him forever is the sacrifice of His Son, Jesus. However, those who persist in their unbelief and rebellion will not escape judgment.

SATURDAY, June 10.   Matt. 5:31-37.

Understanding God's laws. Love, truthfulness, and faithfulness are a part of all that God does. The instructions given by Him to His people have their best interest in mind. Where hostility has taken root in relationships, He desires reconciliation. His love, truthfulness, faithfulness, and forgiveness should shine through the lives of His people.

SUNDAY, June 11.   Matt. 5:17-18, 21-22, 27-28, 38-39, 43-44.

God's standard for His kingdom. You would not expect to find rooms filled with spiderwebs, dirty closets, and filthy floors inside a building that is beautifully decorated on the outside. That description, however, is not too far off from depicting the spiritual condition of those who have not trusted Jesus as Saviour. Attempts can be made to beautify one's life on the outside, but only through faith in Jesus are you forgiven of your sins and made beautiful from the inside out.

—Reginald Coats.

LESSON 3   JUNE 18, 2023

Scripture Lesson Text

MARK 3:13 And he goeth up into a mountain, and calleth *unto him* whom he would: and they came unto him.

14 And he ordained twelve, that they should be with him, and that he might send them forth to preach,

15 And to have power to heal sicknesses, and to cast out devils:

16 And Simon he surnamed Peter;

17 And James the *son* of Zebedee, and John the brother of James; and he surnamed them Boanerges, which is, The sons of thunder:

18 And Andrew, and Philip, and Bartholomew, and Matthew, and Thomas, and James the *son* of Alphaeus, and Thaddaeus, and Simon the Canaanite,

19 And Judas Iscariot, which also betrayed him: and they went into an house.

6:6*b* And he went round about the villages, teaching.

7 And he called *unto him* the twelve, and began to send them forth by two and two; and gave them power over unclean spirits;

8 And commanded them that they should take nothing for *their* journey, save a staff only; no scrip, no bread, no money in *their* purse:

9 But *be* shod with sandals; and not put on two coats.

10 And he said unto them, In what place soever ye enter into an house, there abide till ye depart from that place.

11 And whosoever shall not receive you, nor hear you, when ye depart thence, shake off the dust under your feet for a testimony against them. Verily I say unto you, It shall be more tolerable for Sodom and Gomorrha in the day of judgment, than for that city.

12 And they went out, and preached that men should repent.

13 And they cast out many devils, and anointed with oil many that were sick, and healed *them*.

NOTES

A Victorious Kingdom

Lesson Text: Mark 3:13-19; 6:6b-13

Related Scriptures: Matthew 10:1-15; 12:22-32;
Luke 11:14-23; I John 5:14-17

TIME: A.D. 28   PLACES: mountain in Galilee; Galilee

GOLDEN TEXT—"He ordained twelve, that they should be with him, and that he might send them forth to preach" (Mark 3:14).

Lesson Exposition

JESUS CALLED THE TWELVE—Mark 3:13-15

In his parallel text, Luke recorded that Jesus spent the entire night in prayer on a mountain in central Galilee (Luke 6:12-13). The implication is that He spent the night in prayer about the choice of His inner circle of disciples. At the conclusion of His time of prayer, He called the Twelve aside.

Jesus knew His choice of men beforehand and fully understood from the beginning what each of them, including Judas, would bring to His ministry. He would later note that He had full knowledge that Judas was "a devil" (John 6:70).

Of the many people who followed Him, these twelve men would become Jesus' inner circle and His appointed representatives.

Their selection had a twofold purpose. First, they were to be "with him" (Mark 3:14). These were the men who would accompany Him wherever He would go. The people at large would come to recognize them as His apostles, the Twelve, and at times would approach them first when they wanted to see Jesus.

These twelve men would come to know Jesus on a personal and intimate level beyond what others would experience. They would watch Him, study Him, learn from Him, and eventually declare Him to the world. Their deep association with Him would constitute the core of their training.

Jesus' second purpose was for the Twelve to be sent out with a threefold mission. First, they were to carry His message, which they would ultimately do on a grand scale.

Next, they were to be able to demonstrate their message with power over sickness and disease. Just as Jesus had validated His words and His identity with His miracles, so the disciples would validate theirs with supernatural power.

Finally, the disciples would be empowered with authority over the demonic realm. This was their ultimate enemy, and they would need to be able to demonstrate their spiritual power against it.

THE NAMES OF THE TWELVE DISCIPLES—Mark 3:16-19

The first disciple mentioned is Simon, whom Jesus renamed Peter. Peter, or "Cephas" in Aramaic, meant "stone" or "rock" (John 1:42). Peter assumed a leadership role among the disciples both during Jesus' ministry and also in the early church after the Day of Pentecost.

James and John are mentioned next. They were brothers who worked together for their father in the fishing industry on the Sea of Galilee. Jesus gave them the nickname "The sons of thunder" (Mark 3:17). A number of suggestions have been offered for such a nickname. Perhaps either they or their father had a violent temper (Luke 9:54); perhaps they had booming voices, well-suited to preaching; or perhaps their zeal set them apart. There are no conclusive answers.

Andrew was one of the two disciples of John the Baptist who first turned to Jesus (John 1:35-40). It was Andrew who, with his brother Peter and with James and John, was one of the first disciples called by Jesus beside the Sea of Galilee (Matt. 4:18-22).

Jesus had asked Philip to follow Him shortly after His baptism (John 1:43). Not only did Philip follow Him immediately, but he also sought out Nathanael and told him that he had found the Messiah (vs. 45). Philip was from the same hometown as Peter and Andrew (vs. 44).

The next apostle, Bartholomew, may be the same person as Nathanael (21:2). Bartholomew was initially skeptical when Philip told him the Messiah was from Nazareth, but he soon admitted that Jesus was the Son of God and King of Israel (1:45-49). Matthew, also called Levi, was the tax collector whom Jesus called (Mark 2:14). We read his eyewitness account of Jesus' ministry in the Gospel that bears his name.

Thomas is an Aramaic name meaning "twin." Thomas would later prove to be skeptical about the resurrection until he was confronted with the risen Christ face to face (John 20:24-29).

James the son of Alphaeus may have also been known as James the Less and James the Younger. His mother was present at the crucifixion (Mark 15:40). He is an obscure figure whom the Lord used without fanfare or great visibility. In many ways, he may have been like most Christians—content to obey the Lord without a lot of attention.

Thaddaeus is called Labbaeus in Matthew (10:3). Many scholars also identify him as the Judas of Luke 6:16. His obscure character came out of the shadows once when he asked Jesus how He was going to manifest Himself only to the disciples (John 14:22).

Simon the Canaanite is also called Simon Zealot (Acts 1:13). The word "Canaanite" may actually be from an Aramaic term meaning "zealot." Simon could have been one of the Jewish patriots who called themselves the Zealots and wanted to revolt against Rome. It is also possible his name simply refers to his zeal for God.

The final name was Judas Iscariot. "Iscariot" may be a reference to his hometown of Kerioth (cf. Josh. 15:25). Judas was the only disciple not from Galilee. Some have suggested his name comes from the Latin word *sicarius*, which means "assassin." Whatever the case, his name has gone down into history as the one who betrayed Jesus.

JESUS SENT OUT THE TWELVE— Mark 6:6*b*-13

Jesus sent His disciples by twos (Mark 6:6*b*-7). Jesus continued His traveling ministry. Now, however, He was constantly accompanied by His twelve disciples-in-training.

The Twelve were also called apostles (Matt. 10:2). "Apostle" refers to one who is an ambassador or envoy, a messenger sent with a message. It is a reference to a person who is sent with the full authority of the person he represents.

The disciples were sent out in groups of two as they applied what Jesus had taught them. In the Old Testament, the testimony of at least two witnesses was required to establish a matter (Deut. 17:6). By traveling in pairs, they could also provide prayer, encouragement, and support for one another.

Jesus also sent them armed with the power they would need to overcome unclean spirits. Jesus was able to transfer authority and power to His disciples.

The disciples were to take no provisions (Mark 6:8-10). While Jesus provided His disciples with spiritual power, He intentionally had them limit themselves in their physical provisions. They were not to be burdened with supplies. They were to depend in faith upon God and the goodwill of others for food and shelter. This is the way Jesus Himself conducted His ministry.

The disciples were to establish a base of operations in a community. They were to find and remain in a suitable home until their mission was done. Their urgent work was not to be overshadowed by material concerns.

Jesus' warning for those who would reject the disciples (Mark 6:11). Jesus gave a stern warning for those homes or villages that might reject the disciples. Since they were representatives of Christ and proclaimers of His message, rejection of them was a rejection of Him.

If the gospel was rejected, the disciples were to shake the dust of that village off their feet. This was a symbolic act. In this case, it served as a notice of the village's rejection of the gospel. This "is a public declaration of the divine displeasure that rests on a place that has refused the gospel" (Hendrickson, *Exposition of the Gospel According to Mark,* Baker).

The disciples would have carried out their duties to the village, but the village would have made its decision to reject their message. The people would have to answer to God, who would judge them harshly.

The success of the mission (Mark 6:12-13). The disciples carried out their assignments successfully. The message of the gospel went forth, demons were cast out, and those who were sick were healed. This was a crucial lesson for the Twelve.

The disciples not only succeeded as ambassadors but also were able to see for themselves the power of Christ in them, His representatives.

—*Carter Corbrey.*

PRACTICAL POINTS

1. Jesus Himself selected the twelve disciples (Mark 3:13-14).
2. Believers are to spend time getting to know Jesus.
3. Jesus empowers believers for their tasks (vss. 14-15).
4. The disciples were important because of how each related to Christ (vss. 16-19).
5. Jesus carried out His ministry in an organized fashion (6:6).
6. The disciples did not go out by themselves but by twos (vs. 7).
7. Jesus' followers are not to depend on themselves (vss. 8-9).
8. The disciples were to depend on the kindness of others for their provisions (vs. 10).
9. When someone rejects Christ and His messengers, he can expect only judgment (vs. 11).
10. Obedience to Jesus will result in a successful ministry (vss. 12-13).

—*Carter Corbrey.*

FOR DAILY MEDITATION

MONDAY, June 12.   Matt. 12:22-32.

A house divided. The thought of someone evicting himself from his own house is absurd, and so was the accusation that Jesus casted out demons by the power of Satan. The Pharisees were blinded by their unwillingness to see and acknowledge the truth that was right before their eyes—Jesus is the Messiah. Many people still reject Jesus as Saviour today, but we should still share the gospel with them and pray that God's Spirit would work in their hearts.

TUESDAY, June 13.   Luke 11:14-23.

Jesus overpowers Satan. The devil is a powerful being, but only God is all-powerful. Although Jesus is fully God and fully man, He relied on the power of His Father in heaven during His ministry on earth. Satan and his demons are utterly powerless against God and totally subject to His authority. Those who trust Jesus as their Saviour are forgiven of their sins and delivered into the kingdom of God, and there is nothing that Satan can do about it.

WEDNESDAY, June 14.   I John 5:14-17.

Sin that leads to death. The newness that God brings about in our lives after we have trusted Jesus for salvation also results in a change of attitude. Our hearts become more closely aligned with His, and we should regard sin as He does. While God loves us beyond measure, we should not think that persistently living in a way that takes His grace and mercy for granted does not carry lasting consequences.

THURSDAY, June 15.   Matt. 10:1-15.

The Twelve are sent. Well before commissioning His disciples to take the good news of His death and resurrection to the entire world, Jesus sent His twelve apostles on a mission to tell the people of Israel that the kingdom of heaven was near. Their message was validated by the power given to them by the Lord to work miracles. Today, God's power works the miracle of bringing people back to life spiritually every time Jesus is trusted as Saviour.

FRIDAY, June 16.   Luke 10:1-12.

The seventy-two sent. When Jesus sent a group of seventy-two disciples out, He sent them in groups of two. No one would be on his mission alone. The Lord knows the importance of having someone there to encourage and help you along the way. His Spirit lives in and is with all who trust Jesus as Saviour. No matter how you are feeling, God's Word promises that you are never alone.

SATURDAY, June 17.   Luke 6:1-5.

Lord of the Sabbath. Following religious rules apart from actually knowing and following the Lord was a problem for the Pharisees. Their emphasis was on appearing to love God outwardly, while inwardly they did not even have a relationship with Him. Jesus is Lord of all, including the Sabbath, and He should be given the highest regard and praise in all things.

SUNDAY, June 18.   Mark 3:13-19; 6:6*b*-13.

Authority over Satan. The devil's power is limited, and the time of his evil influence in the world is running out. God's kingdom will be free from Satan's dominion. The Lord's power and authority encompass Satan, demons, and everything else there is. Giving a foretaste of what is yet to come when He reigns forever, Jesus gave His twelve apostles the power to cast out demons. We can rejoice now, knowing that we will one day be delivered from the presence of evil.

—*Reginald Coats.*

Scripture Lesson Text

MATT. 13:24 Another parable put he forth unto them, saying, The kingdom of heaven is likened unto a man which sowed good seed in his field:

25 **But while men slept, his enemy came and sowed tares among the wheat, and went his way.**

26 But when the blade was sprung up, and brought forth fruit, then appeared the tares also.

27 **So the servants of the householder came and said unto him, Sir, didst not thou sow good seed in thy field? from whence then hath it tares?**

28 He said unto them, An enemy hath done this. The servants said unto him, Wilt thou then that we go and gather them up?

29 **But he said, Nay; lest while ye gather up the tares, ye root up also the wheat with them.**

30 Let both grow together until the harvest: and in the time of harvest I will say to the reapers, Gather ye together first the tares, and bind them in bundles to burn them: but gather the wheat into my barn.

31 **Another parable put he forth unto them, saying, The kingdom of heaven is like to a grain of mustard seed, which a man took, and sowed in his field:**

32 Which indeed is the least of all seeds: but when it is grown, it is the greatest among herbs, and becometh a tree, so that the birds of the air come and lodge in the branches thereof.

33 **Another parable spake he unto them; The kingdom of heaven is like unto leaven, which a woman took, and hid in three measures of meal, till the whole was leavened.**

NOTES

Growing God's Kingdom

Lesson Text: Matthew 13:24-33

Related Scriptures: Daniel 2:24-47; Matthew 13:36-43;
Mark 4:26-32; Luke 13:18-21

TIME: A.D. 28   PLACE: by the Sea of Galilee

GOLDEN TEXT—"Let both grow together until the harvest: and in the time of harvest I will say to the reapers, Gather ye together first the tares, and bind them in bundles to burn them: but gather the wheat into my barn" (Matthew 13:30).

Lesson Exposition

Anyone who pays attention to the news, even to a small degree, can plainly see what the world is like. Corruption, terrorism, racism, genocide, slavery, abuse, poverty, and a host of other conditions litter the global landscape, and those of us who believe the Bible and who want God to intervene are having a hard time waiting. Clearly, the kingdoms of this world are not worthy to be compared to the kingdom of our God. Scripture may not give us a lot of detail about God's kingdom, but we certainly have enough information to make us long for it, even to pray, "Thy kingdom come. Thy will be done in earth, as it is in heaven" (Matt. 6:10).

Jesus spoke often about the kingdom, and much of what He said was couched in parables. The word "parable" literally means "to set alongside," thus a story that makes a comparison. It is the verbal painting of a picture. When the Jewish people showed little or no interest in what Jesus was plainly saying, He turned to the use of parables, which, in a way, shielded information from them (13:11, 34-35). He did, however, give explanations to those who asked for clarification, as His disciples often did. This week, we are looking at three of His parables dealing with God's just kingdom.

THE WHEAT AND THE TARES— Matt. 13:24-30

The sowing (Matt. 13:24-25). Using a situation the people of an agrarian society could identify with, Jesus told of a landowner who planted good seed in his field. Once the sowing was complete, he rested from his labor. While the farmer slept, his enemy came to the same piece of land and sowed bad seed. At this point, the sower is not identified, and a motive is not given for the despicable act of the enemy. More information will be given later when Jesus' disciples ask for an explanation (vss. 36-43).

The harvesting (Matt. 13:26-30). With the passing of time, the result of the enemy's work became evident. It should be noted here that the bad seeds sown by the enemy are called "tares," weeds that bear a strong resemblance to wheat until the heads form, whereupon the difference becomes more noticeable. The servants of the landowner saw what had happened, notified their master, and questioned whether they should go through the field and weed out the tares. Out of concern for the wheat, the farmer told them to leave things as they were so as not to disrupt the crop he had sown. The separation would occur at the time of harvest.

When the background text is consulted, one can clearly see that the kingdom is populated by two kinds of people, those belonging to Jesus and those belonging to the devil. Harvesttime (the end of the world) will be a time of judgment, and the tares will be gathered and destroyed, but the wheat will remain.

While the parable is speaking more about the world as a whole and not specifically the church, there is application for believers today because the church is in the world, and often, the world is in the church. That is to say that in the church, one will find both those who know the Lord and those who are professing Christians only. They may dress alike, look alike, use the same terminology in prayer and conversation, do good deeds side by side, and yet one is bound for glory and the other is not.

The apostle Paul wrote of such things happening when he said, "For such are false apostles, deceitful workers, transforming themselves into the apostles of Christ. And no marvel; for Satan himself is transformed into an angel of light" (II Cor. 11:13-14). Anyone familiar with cults knows that some members use the Bible, at least to a point, and may look and sound like true believers in Christ, but they really have no place for His deity and saving work in their theology, especially regarding the plan of salvation.

Christology, the doctrine of Christ, is always the bellwether that exposes a cult for what it is. Every cult denies the deity of Christ. Whatever their other beliefs, no cult can abide the view that Jesus Christ is God in human form. This is, in fact, what defines a particular group as a cult.

So, not only is the world filled with those of the devil, but even in religious circles, he has made inroads (cf. Jude 1:3-4) and is deceiving many. Let each believer stand firm on the Bible, being God's Word and Jesus Christ, being the only way to the Father, while patiently waiting for God to separate the wheat from the tares on the Day of Judgment.

We need to add here that though there will be an earthly kingdom of God when Jesus returns to establish it, there is in the meantime a kingdom for true believers who have already made Jesus their King and who seek to serve Him and live accordingly. As a true believer's salvation is already in hand— although the fullness of his salvation awaits his entry into glory (Rom. 8:23)—so the kingdom is here for the believer now, though a literal earthly kingdom will also be a reality in the future.

THE MUSTARD SEED—
Matt. 13:31-32

This parable teaches that the kind of full-blown kingdom the Jews expected to see when Messiah came would not appear overnight. It had small beginnings. As the mustard seed is tiny and easily overlooked, so was the beginning of the kingdom: started by One, continued by twelve, and since then joined by millions in successive generations as it grows into a worldwide phenomenon. Though it is true that there are many places in the world where believers number few or none, still the growth of what Jesus began two thousand years ago continues and eventually will be worldwide.

How much of your life have you given to Jesus? How closely are you following His Word, and in what way are you helping the spread of the gospel message? Even though some may be quite limited due to age or health reasons, it is not too late to make some adjustments. The Lord will surely bless those who do what they can out of loyalty to Him.

THE LEAVEN—Matt. 13:33

Leaven, or yeast, is often used in the Bible (but not always) to represent evil in the world. The context determines its meaning—as in this parable. Today's cook will put yeast into dough when making bread, but in Bible times cooks would take a piece of pre-leavened dough and insert it into new dough, allowing its leavening effect to gradually spread throughout the loaf.

With this illustration, Jesus taught much the same truth as the preceding parable: the fact that the kingdom would not come with great pomp, pageantry, and ceremony. Time and patience would be needed, but it would surely come.

To repeat and sum up, we see that Jesus was trying to correct the understanding of the Jews of His day as to the timing and nature of God's kingdom. They wanted Rome to be overthrown and the kingdom restored to Israel. In essence, they sought a political kingdom. That was why they turned on Jesus so quickly after His triumphal entry when they saw that He was not going to do what they wanted Him to do (John 19:14-15; cf. 6:15).

How quickly do we become disappointed with the Lord when prayer is not answered immediately or when life just seems to be so against us? We all have our ideas as to who Jesus is, what He can do, and what He should do. When our expectations are not fulfilled, it can be discouraging, and maybe for some, even devastating.

We all likely suffer at least minicrises in faith, and the best thing we can do when that happens is to reinstall Jesus as King of our lives and get back to being His obedient subjects, saying, "Not my will, but thine, be done" (Luke 22:42). The promises of God were given for a purpose too, so we ought not neglect them. We do not know the immediate future, but we know our King, and we know our ultimate destination is in His eternal kingdom.

—Darrell W. McKay.

PRACTICAL POINTS

1. Parables are down-to-earth stories that reveal spiritual truths to those of us with ears to hear (Matt. 13:24).
2. We need to be alert to the fact that not every person professing Jesus is a true believer (vss. 25-28).
3. The church needs to judge itself and test those who seem Christlike, knowing that in the end it is God who makes final judgment (vss. 29-30).
4. As we witness to others, we join the Lord in the work of building His church (vss. 31-32).
5. We must be patient for the gospel message to permeate the hearts and minds of the unsaved (vs. 33).
6. Our part in kingdom work is to spread the gospel throughout the world.

—Darrell W. McKay.

FOR DAILY MEDITATION

MONDAY, June 9.   Mark 4:26-32.

Small beginnings. God can do much with little. Actually, He can take nothing and create an entire universe. Our all-powerful God also causes His kingdom to flourish by using what many regard as insignificant—the good news of His Son, Jesus. Every time that you share or help someone understand the gospel of Jesus Christ, the kingdom of God is being spread through you. God does big things through our little lives.

TUESDAY, June 20.   Luke 13:18-21.

Increasing influence. A tiny mustard seed can be difficult to see. After being planted and given time, however, what began as miniscule grows to become magnificent. Such is the case with God's kingdom as He works in and through the hearts and lives of those who turn to Him for salvation. The influence of God through His people will continue to spread until King Jesus returns and is recognized and acknowledged as Lord by all the earth.

WEDNESDAY, June 21.   Dan. 2:24-47.

Setting up God's kingdom. As powerful and numerous as ancient kingdoms and empires have been, they have all come to an end. Although power is something that so many desperately strive for and are seldom willing to relinquish once they have obtained it, God's kingdom is the only one that will last forever. We can confidently look forward to the time when all this world's misuse and abuse of power is brought to an end. Christ will reign in perfect righteousness and with the full power and authority of God.

THURSDAY, June 22.   Matt. 24:29-31.

The returning Christ. In spite of signs, such as giving sight to the blind and raising the dead, that were done by Jesus during His earthly ministry, many of the Jewish religious leaders demanded a sign from heaven, indicating that He was indeed the Messiah. His return will be accompanied by an unmistakable sign, and the whole world will eventually see that Jesus is Israel's promised Messiah and the Saviour of all who have put their faith in Him.

FRIDAY, June 23.   Matt. 13:36-43.

Evil removed from the world. Inward motives can be disguised by outward appearances. In the present world, those who belong to the Lord through faith in Jesus Christ live alongside those who belong to the devil. God fully knows who does and does not have a relationship with Him through faith in His Son. The world's evil intentions can be craftily directed at God's people, but He will one day deliver us from the presence of all that is evil and corrupt.

SATURDAY, June 24.   Rev. 14:14-20.

The final harvest. All rebellion against the Lord will eventually be brought to an end. His mercy and patience are presently being demonstrated through the withholding of His final judgment. However, there will be no escape for His enemies when Christ returns. In the meantime, God's people can pray that He would soften the hearts of those who are currently fighting against Him.

SUNDAY, June 25.   Matt. 13:24-33.

Good and evil grow together. Good and evil can exist together in the world, but that will not be the case in heaven. Relying on the Lord's strength to overcome evil with good can seem like a daunting challenge, but you should be encouraged to know that living with the Lord, apart from all current cares and concerns, awaits each of God's children.

—*Reginald Coats.*

Scripture Lesson Text

LUKE 11:1 And it came to pass, that, as he was praying in a certain place, when he ceased, one of his disciples said unto him, Lord, teach us to pray, as John also taught his disciples.

2 And he said unto them, When ye pray, say, Our Father which art in heaven, Hallowed be thy name. Thy kingdom come. Thy will be done, as in heaven, so in earth.

3 Give us day by day our daily bread.

4 And forgive us our sins; for we also forgive every one that is indebted to us. And lead us not into temptation; but deliver us from evil.

5 And he said unto them, Which of you shall have a friend, and shall go unto him at midnight, and say unto him, Friend, lend me three loaves;

6 For a friend of mine in his journey is come to me, and I have nothing to set before him?

7 And he from within shall answer and say, Trouble me not: the door is now shut, and my children are with me in bed; I cannot rise and give thee.

8 I say unto you, Though he will not rise and give him, because he is his friend, yet because of his importunity he will rise and give him as many as he needeth.

9 And I say unto you, Ask, and it shall be given you; seek, and ye shall find; knock, and it shall be opened unto you.

10 For every one that asketh receiveth; and he that seeketh findeth; and to him that knocketh it shall be opened.

11 If a son shall ask bread of any of you that is a father, will he give him a stone? or if *he ask* a fish, will he for a fish give him a serpent?

12 Or if he shall ask an egg, will he offer him a scorpion?

13 If ye then, being evil, know how to give good gifts unto your children: how much more shall *your* heavenly Father give the Holy Spirit to them that ask him?

NOTES

Praying to God

Lesson Text: Luke 11:1-13

Related Scriptures: Exodus 16:15-22; Matthew 6:5-15; Romans 8:14-17, 26-27; I John 1:5-10

TIME: A.D. 29   PLACE: Judea

GOLDEN TEXT—"When ye pray, say, Our Father which art in heaven, Hallowed be thy name. Thy kingdom come. Thy will be done, as in heaven, so in earth" (Luke 11:2).

Lesson Exposition

Jesus taught His disciples how to pray. Christ gave them a model prayer. He followed with a parable to encourage them to be persistent in praying. He assured them that prayer was effective. The Father knows how to respond to His children's prayers with good gifts.

INSTRUCTIONS ON PRAYER— Luke 11:1-4

The occasion (Luke 11:1). While Jesus was praying, one of His disciples was deeply impressed with the way in which He was doing it. Jesus was a man of prayer (cf. 3:21; 6:12). When He finished praying, the disciple asked Him to teach them how to pray. John the Baptist had taught his disciples to pray, so this disciple desired the same instructions from Christ.

The foundation (Luke 11:2). Jesus responded by giving them a model prayer. His words "When ye pray, say" meant "This is how you should pray." This model prayer was not to be thoughtlessly repeated (cf. Matt. 6:7). It provides an outline for our prayers.

Jesus taught that prayer is to be directed to the Heavenly Father. His model prayer expresses the disciples' dependence on God. "Our Father" (Luke 11:2) signifies a relationship established by faith. With the use of this intimate and respectful term of address, the Son of God expressed His own unique relationship to God.

Through His redemptive death on the cross, Jesus brought about our reconciliation with God. We have become God's spiritual children. We now address the Father as "our Father" (cf. John 20:17; Rom. 8:15-16).

At the heart of our praying is that God's name would be honored as holy. The term "hallowed" means holy (Luke 11:2). God's name should be honored throughout the world for who He is (Pss. 72:19; 99:1-3). His name is set apart from all other names, for there is no other god like our Heavenly Father.

Because we desire God to be glorified, we long for the Father's kingdom to come so that His will comes to fruition on earth. Christ's disciples should long for the day when He returns. Then Christ will rule and reign over all the earth (Pss. 2:6-9; 72:1, 7- 8). All power and authority will be placed under His feet (I Cor. 15:24-26). The Father's will shall be done on earth just as it is done in heaven.

The resulting petitions (Luke 11:3-4). We are to be sure to ask for daily food. "Give" is in the present tense, so the request is for God to keep giving. The request could be paraphrased "Keep giving us the food that we need for each day." To trust God for sufficient food day by day was especially important to people in Jesus' time. People were often hired and paid only a day at a time (cf. Matt. 20:1-2).

The next petition is for the forgiveness of sins. The Father forgives us on the basis of Christ's redemptive death (Eph. 1:7). The connection between this request and the willingness to forgive others is essential. It shows that what a disciple asks of God, he should be ready to do as well (Luke 6:37). We are to be ready to forgive those who have incurred a debt through sinning against us.

The next petition is that the Father will not lead us into temptation. This does not imply that God might otherwise lure us to do evil. God does not entice us to sin (Jas. 1:13). But He does allow His people's faithfulness to be tested (vss. 2-4, 12). This prayer asks for divine help to not succumb to sin's power when we are being tested. When asked, the Father will provide strength so that circumstances will not overwhelm a believer (I Cor. 10:13).

PARABLE ON PRAYER—
Luke 11:5-8

Christ gave a parable to illustrate the certainty of receiving an answer to prayer.

The urgent request (Luke 11:5-6). Christ asked His disciples a question. Suppose one of them would go to a neighbor at midnight to borrow three loaves of bread. The bread was needed because a guest had arrived very late. Hospitality was considered an obligation, even a sacred duty, for any host in the ancient Near East. The man needed to feed the traveler who had come to spend the night. He may not have been expecting him, and he had used up all that day's bread by nightfall.

The night arrival was unusual, since travel was almost always done during the daylight hours. The host was expected to provide a welcome meal. This host did the only thing he knew to do, which was to seek the help of his neighbor. He hoped that his neighbor had a good supply of bread.

The response (Luke 11:7-8). The friend's reply was no. The door was shut, which meant that he and his children were in bed for the night. He could not get up and give his friend bread. The scene here is a typical Palestinian home. The family is asleep in one room. This was probably the only room in the house. The family would sleep together on one floor mat. His breadless neighbor's request would inconvenience him. He would find it difficult to get over to the door and slide open the heavy lock without waking up his family.

Nevertheless, the neighbor would respond to his friend at the door. He would get up and give his friend as much bread as he needed. He would do so not because of his friendship but because of his friend's "importunity" (vs. 8). This term refers to the persistence of the one knocking at the door. The neighbor gets out of bed, lights a lamp, unlocks and opens the door, and gives his friend all the bread that he needs to be a good host.

The neighbor did not want to be disturbed; but this is not true of God, who eagerly waits to listen to the request of one of His children (vss. 10, 13). This is the main point of the parable. If an unwilling neighbor can be moved by a persistent request, how much more will the Father be moved by persistent intercession? His ears are open to the prayers of believers (I Pet. 3:12). Perseverance in prayer is an evidence of faith and dependence on the Lord.

EFFECTIVENESS OF PRAYER—
Luke 11:9-13

The exhortation and promise (Luke 11:9-10). Christ drove home the point of His parable. He gave a threefold exhortation accompanied by a threefold promise. The threefold exhortation was "ask," "seek," and "knock." These three verbs are in the present tense, referring to continual actions. They are also imperatives. Asking, seeking, and knocking through persistent praying is not an optional thing for believers, for the Father commands these things of us (Matt. 7:7-8; I Thess. 5:17).

The threefold promise means that our persistent request will be granted. Our need will be met. We will find what we have sought. The door of blessing and opportunity will be opened to us. Prayer is purposeful and effective, for God uses prayer to accomplish His purpose. Persistence in prayer is not wringing an answer out of our Father like squeezing out the last drop of water from a damp cloth. He answers our prayers willingly.

The three promises are arranged as they are for emphasis. Not a single believer who obeys the threefold command will be disappointed. An answer to persistent prayer is promised. Asking, seeking, and knocking imply a belief in a personal God with whom we have a relationship.

Our loving Father (Luke 11:11-13). In responding to essential needs, no father would give ridiculous or dangerous things to his children that would harm or injure them. Even evil men know how to respond properly to a son's request.

Our Heavenly Father will do no less for His children than would an earthly father. He gives us good gifts, not things that would imperil or harm us. Further, God is perfect and will do "much more" than sinful men would (vs. 13). He makes provision for His children by granting those things for which they ask, seek, and knock (Matt. 7:11). Specifically, He grants the Holy Spirit in fulfillment of His promise (Luke 24:49; Acts 2:33).

God does "exceeding abundantly above" all that we ask or even think about asking Him (Eph. 3:20). We are dependent on the Lord in prayer, which reminds us of our absolute dependence on Him for everything. Believers are to boldly ask, seek, and knock, and then expect God to answer. Asking and receiving from God is His will for us.

—*Jack Riggs.*

PRACTICAL POINTS

1. Christ impressed upon His disciples the importance of prayer by His own prayer life (Luke 11:1).
2. We are speaking directly and personally to the God of heaven when we pray (vs. 2).
3. We should never trust solely in our earned income instead of God for our daily food (vs. 3).
4. Our forgiveness of others shows that we understand our own forgiveness (vs. 4).
5. God's eagerness to answer prayers encourages us to pray (vss. 5-8).
6. Prayer is an imperative as well as a privilege for believers (vss. 9-10).
7. God always has our best interests in His mind and heart (vss. 11-12).
8. God provides us with all we need to serve Him (vs. 13).

—*Jack Riggs.*

FOR DAILY MEDITATION

MONDAY, June 26. I Chr. 16:23-34.

Song of praise. God's greatness is displayed in so many ways throughout the earth. The appropriate response is to praise Him for His wondrous works and to worship Him for being who and all that He is. Not only are we surrounded by His goodness, but we are also blessed with the assurance of His presence. God's people should be continually praising Him.

TUESDAY, June 27. Ps. 145:1-21.

Extolling the Lord. No matter how much we praise the Lord, it will still fall short of bestowing unto Him what He actually deserves. His love and goodness toward us cannot be measured. Gratitude on par with the extent to which He has blessed us cannot be adequately expressed. To properly praise and thank our God would take forever, and that is how long we look forward to living with Him in His glorious presence.

WEDNESDAY, June 28. Ex. 16:15-22.

Daily bread for Israel. God miraculously provided for His people in the wilderness. Their faith in Him was to be renewed on a daily basis. God still knows what His people need in order to get through each day. Above all, He knows that we need to trust and rely on Him. Even when you do not receive exactly what you have asked of the Lord, trust that He will supply you with the strength or whatever else is needed to endure without it.

THURSDAY, June 29. Ps. 27:7-14.

Seeking the face of the Lord. Being all alone with no one to turn to can bring feelings of despair. But you can always turn to the Lord in your time of need. David found comfort and encouragement by calling on the Lord. God desires to hear from His people whether it be in good times or bad. He is faithfully working to help His people. Take comfort in knowing that you will never face a problem alone as long as you are looking to the Lord for help.

FRIDAY, June 30. Rom. 3:10-20.

All are unrighteous. Sinfulness shows up through people's lives in various ways. There is simply no one other than God who is completely without sin. Only by God's grace does He declare us righteous through our faith in Jesus Christ. We should, therefore, never think too highly of ourselves. Instead, we should look for opportunities to show and share God's truth, love, and grace with others.

SATURDAY, July 1. Matt. 6:5-8.

Honest prayer. God hears the words that come from our mouths, and He also hears the intentions that come from our hearts. Prayer affords us the opportunity to express praise and also our petitions to our almighty God. Praying for others is commendable, but praying with the intention of impressing others misses the mark of having been granted access into the presence of God through prayer. Be sure that your motives when praying are driven by a desire to please and glorify God.

SUNDAY, July 2. Luke 11:1-13.

Teach us to pray. What better teacher could one have than the Lord Himself? When giving His disciples instructions on how to pray, Jesus spoke of God's desire to reward persistence. God does not need to be reminded, or even informed, about our needs. Continuing in prayer, however, makes us to be mindful of our reliance on Him to provide for our needs. Remember to praise and thank the One from whom every good and perfect gift comes.

—Reginald Coats.

LESSON 6 — JULY 9, 2023

SCRIPTURE LESSON TEXT

LUKE 14:7 And he put forth a parable to those which were bidden, when he marked how they chose out the chief rooms; saying unto them,

8 When thou art bidden of any *man* to a wedding, sit not down in the highest room; lest a more honourable man than thou be bidden of him;

9 And he that bade thee and him come and say to thee, Give this man place; and thou begin with shame to take the lowest room.

10 But when thou art bidden, go and sit down in the lowest room; that when he that bade thee cometh, he may say unto thee, Friend, go up higher: then shalt thou have worship in the presence of them that sit at meat with thee.

11 For whosoever exalteth himself shall be abased; and he that humbleth himself shall be exalted.

15 And when one of them that sat at meat with him heard these things, he said unto him, Blessed *is* he that shall eat bread in the kingdom of God.

16 Then said he unto him, A certain man made a great supper, and bade many:

17 And sent his servant at supper time to say to them that were bidden, Come; for all things are now ready.

18 And they all with one *consent* began to make excuse. The first said unto him, I have bought a piece of ground, and I must needs go and see it: I pray thee have me excused.

19 And another said, I have bought five yoke of oxen, and I go to prove them: I pray thee have me excused.

20 And another said, I have married a wife, and therefore I cannot come.

21 So that servant came, and shewed his lord these things. Then the master of the house being angry said to his servant, Go out quickly into the streets and lanes of the city, and bring in hither the poor, and the maimed, and the halt, and the blind.

22 And the servant said, Lord, it is done as thou hast commanded, and yet there is room.

23 And the lord said unto the servant, Go out into the highways and hedges, and compel *them* to come in, that my house may be filled.

24 For I say unto you, That none of those men which were bidden shall taste of my supper.

NOTES

Accept God's Invitation!

Lesson Text Luke 14:7-11, 15-24

Related Scriptures: Proverbs 25:6-7; Matthew 21:42-44; 22:1-14

TIME: A.D. 30   PLACE: Perea

GOLDEN TEXT—"And the lord said unto the servant, Go out into the highways and hedges, and compel them to come in, that my house may be filled" (Luke 14:23).

Lesson Exposition

Before Jesus began telling the parable in this week's lesson, Jesus had healed a man who was a fellow guest to the meal. The lawyers and Pharisees had held their peace when Jesus asked a pointed question about the law. Jesus' question was an invitation to the religious leaders to have a better understanding of the heart of God when applying the law in daily life. Their obedience to the law should have come from the same heart of compassion and love that the Lawgiver had.

We are invited to the same. Our favorable response to God's invitation is based on the truth that the final form of His kingdom will be glorious and filled with joy. It will be a place where our weaknesses and imperfections will be no more and where we will rejoice in the presence of a loving and merciful Father. Why not keep these images in mind throughout the coming week, especially as you weigh your response to God and His call on your life?

THE TEACHING ABOUT HUMILITY—Luke 14:7-11

The folly of pride (Luke 14:7-9). On one Sabbath, Jesus was dining in the home of a highly respected Pharisee (vs. 1). Before the meal began, Jesus had noticed that the dinner guests endeavored to sit in the places of honor. Apparently, this particular banquet was a rather important occasion, and everybody desired to be seen as being among those of special distinction.

When Jesus began to tell the parable, everyone had been seated, so it was doubtful anything would change for the current event, but His story may have given those in attendance pause when attending the next event. It may be that Jesus found the whole spectacle amusing and telling of the condition of their hearts. They were putting their own interests above others, revealing an attitude of pride that a guest would assume he or she is the most important person in the room.

Jesus stated that it was unwise to be bold enough to sit in a place of honor, for an occasion might arise in which someone with more prestige showed up later at the banquet. Imagine the embarrassment felt by the presumptuous attendee when the host asked him to move to some other spot at the end of the table to make room for the more distinguished guest!

Not that we today are any different, for we often look for subtle, and not-so-subtle, ways for self-promotion. What are some ways that we let others know about our goodness or our talents in a way that is only self-serving instead of letting God promote us?

The wisdom of humility (Luke 14:10-11). Jesus' recommendation must have seemed counterintuitive to His listeners; nevertheless, it resonated with the divine priority to cultivate humility rather than pride. Jesus encouraged sitting down at the lowest place of the table and perhaps being invited by the host to move up higher.

To further emphasize His point, Jesus declared, "Whosoever exalteth himself shall be abased; and he that humbleth himself shall be exalted" (vs. 11). This is about as countercultural as one can get. In a world of selfies and social-media influencers, self-promotion is the only way to success.

The guests were not the only ones Jesus addressed. He had a message of humility for the hosts too. He challenged those in attendance to extend invitations to those who would not be able to reciprocate. In this, the host would be a blessing to others. In turn, God would bless the host.

Jesus explained that in the Day of Judgment, those who were proud in this life will be humbled; in contrast, those who were humble will be exalted. The context strongly suggests that it is God who will do the exalting or humbling.

THE PARABLE ABOUT THE GREAT BANQUET—Luke 14:15-24

An attendee's exclamation (Luke 14:15). In response to Jesus' admonition to hosts, another guest declared to Jesus that those who will get to feast in the kingdom of God are blessed. The statement may have been an attempt to impress Jesus.

In reply, Jesus told a story illustrating how the guests who eventually will attend the heavenly banquet are not necessarily the ones who were expected.

A spurned invitation (Luke 14:16-20). On the surface, Jesus' parable is simple. Yet in response to the proclamation in verse 15, it may have been a way to teach those in attendance how one truly becomes a member of God's kingdom.

In Jesus' story, a man plans a large dinner and makes certain that his friends are notified beforehand. As it is today, it would have been normal to invite people well in advance of the party.

When the time comes for the actual meal, he sends his servant to alert the guests. It was customary at that time for a second invitation to be given once the meal was ready. A servant would be dispatched to remind the guests of their earlier commitment.

In the same way, many announcements were made to the Jewish people that the Messiah was coming and that they should be getting ready for His arrival. These announcements were received and accepted gladly. No one knew the exact time of the Messiah's arrival, but it was considered good news that He was coming to provide deliverance for His people. The people of Israel thought they were ready.

In Jesus' parable, though, these guests shockingly declined to come as promised. One invited guest declined and sent regrets because he wanted to check out a newly purchased piece of land. Another preferred to test five teams of oxen that he had just bought. The third chose to stay home with his new bride. Not one of these excuses was adequate to justify breaking a commitment to attend the feast. Every one smacked of insincerity. Each person had a preoccupation with other things that he considered more important than the dinner.

With this story, Jesus was suggesting to the Pharisees around the table that they had much in common with the three invited guests. Although they expressed their devotion at every opportunity and heartily endorsed the prospect of an eternity with God, Jesus knew that at the same time they were finding reasons why they would not be able to attend His own banquet—the feast of salvation.

An expanded invitation to others (Luke 14:21-24). When the host learned from his servant that his invited guests would not be coming, he became angry. If they had no desire to be with him, he would open his doors to those who would welcome his invitation. After all, the food was prepared and the table set. It should not go to waste.

Instead of leading a dinner party for the well-known and well-to-do, the host called in the outcasts of society. In Israel, it was the religious leaders who first rejected Jesus and eventually saw to His death. They had an opportunity to receive Him but refused. Since the religious leaders showed no interest in spiritual truth, Jesus went directly to the people with His teaching.

In Jesus' parable, the servant reported to his master that he had done as he was told. Even after his new guests were gathered, though, there was still room for more at the banquet. The host thus gave a second call, inviting whomever he might gather from some distance away.

Persuasion rather than brute force is implied in the phrase "compel [people] to come in" (vs. 23). Food, drink, and fellowship would be powerful incentives for needy folks. From this, we see that the Lord offers us blessings greater than anything the world has to offer.

Jesus was speaking quite clearly to His host and the other guests. They were the ones who should have embraced Him—the ones who were best equipped to understand exactly who He was and what His coming meant for Israel and the world; but they would not have Him. Jesus would therefore invite to salvation those who were willing to come when He called. We too should willingly reach out with the good news to everyone we can. It is of utmost urgency that they come.

—*Dan Lioy.*

PRACTICAL POINTS

1. When we put the concerns of others ahead of our wishes and preferences, God is pleased (Luke 14:7).
2. It is more honorable to be promoted than demoted before one's peers (vss. 8-9).
3. God has a way of humbling the proud while at the same time lifting up the humble (vss. 10-11).
4. Those who humbly trust in Christ for salvation are the ones who will enjoy the endless fellowship of God's coming rule (vs. 15).
5. Rather than come humbly before the throne of God's grace, the unsaved make excuses as to why they cannot do so (vss. 16-20).
6. There is more than enough room in the kingdom of God for every repentant sinner (vss. 21-22).
7. The Lord wants all people to be saved and come to know the truth (Luke 14:23-24; cf. II Pet. 3:9).

—*Dan Lioy.*

FOR DAILY MEDITATION

MONDAY, July 3.   Matt. 22:1-14.

Unprepared for the kingdom. The good news of Jesus' death, burial, and resurrection is powerful enough to save all that believe. No matter what one's status is in society or what prestigious positions one might hold, accepting God's invitation through faith in Jesus is the only way into His kingdom. Those who trust Jesus as Saviour are clothed in His righteousness, but those who do not trust Him remain unprepared and unfit for God's kingdom.

TUESDAY, July 4.   Matt. 21:42-44.

The Stone rejected. The rejection of Jesus as Messiah by the majority of the people of Israel did not thwart but rather advanced God's redemptive plan. Jesus' rejection and subsequent death and resurrection were always the foundation upon which God's church would be established. The Old Testament Scriptures anticipated Jesus' coming, and those who reject Him do so to their own detriment. God's plan will always prevail.

WEDNESDAY, July 5.   Acts 13:44-52.

Gospel scorned by the Jews. Jesus and His first followers were Jewish. The overwhelming majority of Jewish religious leaders, however, stood in opposition to Jesus' followers spreading the good news of His death, burial, and resurrection. In spite of rejection and opposition, God has ensured that the message of forgiveness through faith in Jesus as Saviour has continued to spread. Pray that the gospel would continue to reach new people groups.

THURSDAY, July 6.   Prov. 25:6-7.

A place of honor. The trait of humility should be exhibited through the lives of God's people. We are constantly in need of His sustaining power, and to think or act otherwise would be extremely foolish. Praising God for all that He has done and deserves should leave no room for pride. Any sense of superiority will eventually be humbled and will result in embarrassment. The highest praise, honor, and glory belongs to the Lord our God.

FRIDAY, July 7.   Isa. 2:10-12.

The proud will be humbled. Being proud can lead to refusing help and even willfully ignoring one's need for it. Instead of turning to and trusting the Lord with faith, the sinful and proud of this world reject the truth of His Word while relying on their own cleverness and ability to reason. God's judgment, however, will cause terror and bring the pride of the proud crashing down. In the end, all will see and acknowledge that the Lord is the Most High God.

SATURDAY, July 8.   Luke 14:12-14.

Hospitality to the poor. Some people do favors for others only with the expectation of having their *acts* of kindness reciprocated. But this is not the manner in which God bestows His favor on us and neither should it be the attitude in our hearts. God gives of Himself and His goodness freely. How might you show God's kindness to someone who is unable to repay you?

SUNDAY, July 9.   Luke 14:7-11, 15-24.

Two critical warnings. There is a stark difference between being honored in the eyes of the world and being honored in the eyes of God. Jesus told a parable about a wedding feast and another about a great banquet to drive home the importance of humility. Only after recognizing and admitting our spiritual poverty are we fit for God's kingdom. By His grace and through faith in His Son, we are exalted by God and receive honored status in His kingdom.

—*Reginald Coats.*

LESSON 7   JULY 16, 2023

Scripture Lesson Text

LUKE 16:19 There was a certain rich man, which was clothed in purple and fine linen, and fared sumptuously every day:

20 And there was a certain beggar named Lazarus, which was laid at his gate, full of sores,

21 And desiring to be fed with the crumbs which fell from the rich man's table: moreover the dogs came and licked his sores.

22 And it came to pass, that the beggar died, and was carried by the angels into Abraham's bosom: the rich man also died, and was buried;

23 And in hell he lift up his eyes, being in torments, and seeth Abraham afar off, and Lazarus in his bosom.

24 And he cried and said, Father Abraham, have mercy on me, and send Lazarus, that he may dip the tip of his finger in water, and cool my tongue; for I am tormented in this flame.

25 But Abraham said, Son, remember that thou in thy lifetime receivedst thy good things, and likewise Lazarus evil things: but now he is comforted, and thou art tormented.

26 And beside all this, between us and you there is a great gulf fixed: so that they which would pass from hence to you cannot; neither can they pass to us, that *would come* from thence.

27 Then he said, I pray thee therefore, father, that thou wouldest send him to my father's house:

28 For I have five brethren; that he may testify unto them, lest they also come into this place of torment.

29 Abraham saith unto him, They have Moses and the prophets; let them hear them.

30 And he said, Nay, father Abraham: but if one went unto them from the dead, they will repent.

31 And he said unto him, If they hear not Moses and the prophets, neither will they be persuaded, though one rose from the dead.

NOTES

A Warning for the Hard-Hearted

Lesson Text: Luke 16:19-31

Related Scriptures: Matthew 6:19-20;
Hebrews 3:7-19; Revelation 20:11-15; 21:5-8

TIME: A.D. 30   PLACE: probably Perea

GOLDEN TEXT—"Son, remember that thou in thy lifetime receivedst thy good things, and likewise Lazarus evil things: but now he is comforted, and thou art tormented" (Luke 16:25).

Lesson Exposition

A preliminary word about the parable we are about to study is in order, since, if taken by itself, it would seem to teach salvation by works. That would go against the teaching of Scripture (John 3:16; 14:6; Acts 2:21; 16:30-31; Eph. 2:8-9), which makes it clear that repentant faith in the Lord Jesus Christ is required to be saved. So at the outset, it should be established that the parable is not teaching salvation by works.

This parable closes a chapter devoted to the use of money. It began with Jesus, by means of a parable, instructing His disciples on using money wisely, followed by the comment that man "cannot serve God and mammon" (Luke 16:13). Then, not surprisingly, we discover the Pharisees were also listening to Jesus.

Being lovers of money themselves, and upon hearing what Jesus said about its use, they loudly proclaimed their contempt for Him. That turned the Lord's attention to them, and He accused them of not only justifying themselves before others but at the same time also disregarding Scripture (the Law and the Prophets) if it was in their interests. Then He spoke our parable for their benefit. It too is about money. Our unit's theme is on how we are to respond to God's kingdom, and the lesson's theme is those who have hardened their hearts to what it means to live as citizens of God's kingdom.

A TALE OF TWO LIVES—
Luke 16:19-21

A certain rich man (Luke 16:19). Jesus used the same phrase to introduce this parable as He did when He was teaching His disciples (vs. 1). He did not give the man a name, but we are told that the man had great wealth and satisfied his covetous nature by spending it on himself. He wore the best clothing money could buy; only the very rich could afford clothing made with costly purple dye, and his garments were of the finest material that could be obtained. This man dressed in expensive and elegant apparel regularly. One may safely assume he ate nothing but the freshest and finest of food as well and had plenty of it whenever he wanted it.

Likely his description brings to mind images of certain contemporary show-business personalities, business tycoons, or sports stars who seemingly have nothing but money and do not forgo any personal desire. The world certainly has its share of superrich people, but it also has the poor in even greater numbers.

It is difficult for those of us who have grown up in an affluent nation to comprehend the level of destitution that exists in many third-world countries. We must keep in mind that, though we seek to alleviate this suffering where we can, the gospel must remain paramount as we help and assist others.

A certain poor man (Luke 16:20-21). Jesus gave this man the name Lazarus, a Greek name coming from a Hebrew word meaning "helped by God." He may have used the name to show that God recognizes the poor, even if the rich do not. Lazarus could do nothing for himself except ask for the help of others to pick him up and deposit him at the gate of the rich man, who he hoped would have pity on him. This he did regularly. In addition to that, his body had open sores that wild dogs aggravated by licking. The poor man just could not get much of a break. Being sick and immobile, he obviously was dependent on others for everything. The gate of the rich man's house would seem to be the ideal spot to find a bit of relief, but alas, not this rich man.

We may not identify with the rich man and there may not be a beggar at our door, but that does not let us off the hook for using at least part of what we have to lift up those who are in need. It is an investment in the present with rewards in eternity, but it takes open eyes and a compassionate heart, reflecting God Himself.

A TALE OF TWO DEATHS—
Luke 16:22

Very succinctly Jesus said that both the beggar and the rich man died. The former went to heavenly bliss, here called Abraham's bosom, but the only commentary on the rich man's demise was that he was buried.

A TALE OF TWO OUTCOMES—
Luke 16:23-31

The rich man in hell (Luke 16:23). The Greek word for "hell" here is *hades,* which refers to the same place as "Sheol" in the Old Testament and sometimes refers to the grave, or death itself. *Gehenna* is another Greek word translated "hell" and is used when the eternal state of the unsaved is the subject (Matt. 23:15; Luke 12:5). Hades can also be a place of suffering preliminary to hell, as the parable shows. The rich man was in torment amid flames but could see at a distance Abraham and Lazarus. The rich man's immediate need was relief from the heat, and he cried out for mercy, asking Abraham to send Lazarus with even a mere drop of water. The story reveals that the rich man knew Lazarus all along and surely had seen him at his gate many times. The man also thought Lazarus should now serve him.

How many needy do we see at least somewhat regularly or are we aware of through news reports? It is not that we can care for all of them, but do we not have a sense of responsibility to some? Someone once said something to the effect that it is not what we would do if we had a million dollars but what we are doing with the money we have.

The debate with Abraham (Luke 16:24-31). We learn here that after death, people can remember. What a jolting word "remember" must have been for the rich man! Abraham told him to remember the luxurious life he had lived as well as the fact that he never did anything to help Lazarus. He also was told that things had changed. Now he would reap what he had sown. There was finally justice for Lazarus too. The score was settled. When it really mattered, Lazarus won, and the rich man lost.

In addition to all that, it was not possible for Lazarus or anyone to go to the rich man, nor could the rich man or any with him make the opposite journey. Death cements earthly choices. The teaching here is very stark and underlines the necessity of making the right decisions this side of death.

The rich man was aware that he could not go back to family and friends. Suddenly he developed a caring heart, at least for his brothers. He did not want them to make the mistake he had made and end up where he was. He knew he had done wrong, but that knowledge was useless to him where he was, and things would not improve.

Still thinking he could get Abraham and Lazarus to do his bidding, he asked that Lazarus come back from the dead and appear to his brothers, for surely that would bring repentance to them. Jesus closed the parable with a solemn comment that is as true today as the day He told the story. The Word of God (the Law and the Prophets) was available, and it was a better witness than if one rose from the dead. Note the importance and sufficiency of God's Word. People neglect it at their own peril.

To reiterate, the parable does not teach salvation by works but the need for compassion and mercy for one's fellow man—one's neighbor, if you will. To be greedy and uncaring demonstrates a heart that has not been touched by grace and forgiveness. This is the point. It is the gospel that changes an individual and imparts a compassionate heart to those who know the Lord.

The apostle Paul in his epistle to the Colossians urged those who had been saved by grace to put away the old nature and put on the new (Col. 3:8-14). In that passage, the first thing to be put on is called "bowels of mercies," or in today's language, a "heart of compassion." The rich man did not have it toward Lazarus in life and even in death could not bring himself to speak to Lazarus, only to Abraham.

What about us? We must bear in mind that we are saved by grace through faith, but even so, we will stand before Christ and give an answer for the lives we lived as Christians (Rom. 14:10-12). A believer's rewards, or lack thereof in eternity, hinge on what is done with what one has today. It is not too late to get started.

—Darrell W. McKay.

PRACTICAL POINTS

1. Even if we have plenty of this world's goods, it does not mean we should keep them for ourselves (Luke 16:19).
2. If we cannot see the need around us, it may mean that both our heart and our eyes are closed (vss. 20-21).
3. Since death awaits us all, we should prepare for the inevitable (vs. 22).
4. No amount of regret or bargaining after death can change our final destiny (vss. 23-26).
5. The time to be concerned about the future of our loved ones is now. Tomorrow may be too late (vss. 27-28).
6. We need to read and heed the Bible and pray that our loved ones do the same (vss. 29-31).

—Darrell W. McKay.

FOR DAILY MEDITATION

MONDAY, July 10. Matt. 6:19-21.
What does your heart treasure? The pursuit of earthly riches can consume a great deal of time and energy. Instead of prioritizing possessions that are temporary, the Lord would have His people set their hearts on those things that will endure forever. Having material wealth is not sinful of itself, but the love of money should never interfere with or surpass our love for God.

TUESDAY, July 11. Luke 12:32-34.
Give to the poor. Many people turn to safes and vaults to find protection for their riches. But valuables that are protected by such things can still be stolen and destroyed. Trusting the Lord to care for our needs, while also using what He has entrusted into our care for the sake of advancing His kingdom, results in treasure being stored up in heaven.

WEDNESDAY, July 12. Mark 10:17-22.
Heavenly treasure. Complimentary remarks are often met with comments that repay the favor. But the honorable address of the rich man given to Jesus was not enough to bring the affirmation sought by the man. He first needed to truly recognize who Jesus is and to acknowledge his own inability to earn eternal life. Along with the gift of salvation through faith in Jesus Christ, God gives us the opportunity to glorify Him and store up heavenly treasure.

THURSDAY, July 13. Rev. 20:11-15.
Judgment of the dead. There is so much sinfulness in the world, and a great deal of it seems to go unpunished. There will be nowhere to hide, however, for every person who has ever lived, when the time of God's righteous judgment arrives. Those who have died will be resurrected and brought before God for judgment. Having rejected the gift of God's righteousness, which comes through faith in the finished work of Jesus Christ at the cross, unbelievers will be judged and found guilty according to their own unrighteous works.

FRIDAY, July 14. Rev. 21:5-8.
The lake of fire. Those who belong to God through faith in His Son also have His Spirit working in and through their lives. The children of God tend to exhibit a resemblance to their Father in heaven via the godly traits that He produces through their lives. We look forward to a heavenly inheritance while unbelievers, whose lives have a tendency of being marked by ungodly behavior, await an everlasting and fiery judgment.

SATURDAY, July 15. Heb. 3:7-19.
Unbelieving hearts. God has an unblemished track record of keeping His promises. The people of Israel had witnessed His powerful might and faithfulness from up close when He brought the ten plagues upon Egypt. His strength had delivered them, which is why their unbelief such a short time later seems so puzzling. As believers, we need to make sure that we remain just that—*believers* in the Lord and all that He has revealed through His Word.

SUNDAY, July 16. Luke 16:19-31.
The rich man and Lazarus. Current circumstances do not last forever. During his lifetime, the rich man failed to recognize this important truth. His blatant and persistent lack of concern for Lazarus displayed a selfish heart and an unwillingness to do that which is pleasing to the Lord. Lazarus's desperation and affliction were eventually comforted. In the end, it was the rich man who desperately desired to switch places with Lazarus. All our temporary afflictions will be eternally comforted when our trust is in the Lord.
—Reginald Coats.

LESSON 8   JULY 23, 2023

SCRIPTURE LESSON TEXT

MATT. 25:31 When the Son of man shall come in his glory, and all the holy angels with him, then shall he sit upon the throne of his glory:

32 And before him shall be gathered all nations: and he shall separate them one from another, as a shepherd divideth *his* **sheep from the goats:**

33 And he shall set the sheep on his right hand, but the goats on the left.

34 Then shall the King say unto them on his right hand, Come, ye blessed of my Father, inherit the kingdom prepared for you from the foundation of the world:

35 For I was an hungred, and ye gave me meat: I was thirsty, and ye gave me drink: I was a stranger, and ye took me in:

36 Naked, and ye clothed me: I was sick, and ye visited me: I was in prison, and ye came unto me.

37 Then shall the righteous answer him, saying, Lord, when saw we thee an hungred, and fed *thee?* or thirsty, and gave *thee* drink?

38 When saw we thee a stranger, and took *thee* in? or naked, and clothed *thee?*

39 Or when saw we thee sick, or in prison, and came unto thee?

40 And the King shall answer and say unto them, Verily I say unto you, Inasmuch as ye have done *it* unto one of the least of these my brethren, ye have done *it* unto me.

41 Then shall he say also unto them on the left hand, Depart from me, ye cursed, into everlasting fire, prepared for the devil and his angels:

42 For I was an hungred, and ye gave me no meat: I was thirsty, and ye gave me no drink:

43 I was a stranger, and ye took me not in: naked, and ye clothed me not: sick, and in prison, and ye visited me not.

44 Then shall they also answer him, saying, Lord, when saw we thee an hungred, or athirst, or a stranger, or naked, or sick, or in prison, and did not minister unto thee?

45 Then shall he answer them, saying, Verily I say unto you, Inasmuch as ye did *it* not to one of the least of these, ye did *it* not to me.

46 And these shall go away into everlasting punishment: but the righteous into life eternal.

NOTES

Separating the Sheep and the Goats

Lesson Text: Matthew 25:31-46

Related Scriptures: Deuteronomy 15:7-11; Daniel 7:9-14; Matthew 16:24-28; I John 4:7-14

TIME: A.D. 30   PLACE: Jerusalem

GOLDEN TEXT—"And these shall go away into everlasting punishment: but the righteous into life eternal" (Matthew 25:46).

Lesson Exposition

Matthew 24:1 through 25:46 is the last of Jesus' five discourses recorded by Matthew. Because Jesus was sitting on the Mount of Olives when He taught this material to His disciples, it has been called the Olivet Discourse. It contains some of the most noteworthy prophetic passages in all of Scripture.

THE SHEEP AND THE GOATS—Matt. 25:31-33

The coming Judge (Matt. 25:31). In the final parable that Jesus delivered on the Mount of Olives that day, He provided a few details about what His return will be like. First, Jesus will come in glory, or divine splendor, no longer simply appearing as an ordinary man. Second, He will bring with Him all the holy angels, who will no doubt do His bidding. Third, Jesus will sit on His throne in glory, meaning He will rule in splendor.

The determination (Matt. 25:32-33). Once Jesus is seated on His throne, citizens of all the nations will be gathered in His presence. He will then separate the righteous individuals from the wicked. Only God can do that with perfect justice.

Jesus compared the separation of humans to a shepherd's separation of sheep from goats. The sheep and goats were generally separated at the end of the day. As the Shepherd of judgment, Jesus will put the people here represented as sheep on His right (the place of honor in ancient times) and the people represented as goats on His left (the place of dishonor).

THOSE ON CHRIST'S RIGHT—Matt. 25:34-40

The deeds of the blessed (Matt. 25:34-36). To those on His right-hand side, the King will offer an invitation to inherit the kingdom prepared for them by His Father before the creation of the world. The reason the King will give for His invitation is that the righteous loved and took care of Him when He was hungry, thirsty, alone, naked, and imprisoned.

The Lord's response to the questions asked by the blessed (Matt. 25:37-40). Those who are rewarded will not be able to recall a time when they did acts of kindness and compassion for the King. In response to their humble queries, the King will tell them that whatever they did to help the most seemingly insignificant of His followers was likewise done for Him. The divine blessing will thus be given to those who served the needy with no thought of getting a reward. Their service arose from their love and concern for others, not from any desire to receive a reward.

**THOSE ON CHRIST'S LEFT—
Matt. 25:41-46**

The failures of the condemned (Matt. 25:41-43). Jesus next focused on the condemned. Instead of being invited to come, like the ones on the right, the ones on the left will be told to depart. Instead of being blessed by the Father, these people will be cursed. Instead of inheriting the kingdom prepared for the righteous, these people will be consigned to the eternal fire (hell) prepared for Satan and the demons.

Just as the righteous will inherit the kingdom for meeting Jesus' needs, so the wicked will be consigned to hell for not meeting His needs. They will have been presented with the same opportunities to give Him food and drink and rest, but they will have chosen not to do so. For those who spurn Christ, all that remains is for the Lord to condemn them. It will be a terrifying scene as He issues a verdict of guilty against the unsaved.

The Lord's response to the questions asked by the condemned (Matt. 25:44-46). The wicked will be just as mystified as were the righteous about when they had the opportunities that Jesus mentioned. They will ask when they chose not to help the Lord. They did not realize that the basis for judgment will be whether they showed love to others, whom God has created in His image (cf. I John 3:14-18).

Christ's solemn reply will be that refusing to help others in need is the same as refusing to help Him (Matt. 25:45). Verse 46 concludes both the story of the sheep and the story of the goats. The righteous and the wicked have radically different futures. The first group is eternally blessed, while the second group is eternally condemned. Jesus' judgments will be beyond appeal.

We should not interpret the Lord Jesus' parable to mean that one's eternal state is based on good works. Scripture is clear that faith in Christ (or its absence) determines the final end. Nevertheless, we can take away from this parable the ideas that Jesus rewards service done for Him, that real faith is expressed in works, and that He counts service done for His people the same as service done for Him.

—*Dan Lioy.*

PRACTICAL POINTS

1. Those who spurn Christ reject the truth that He will one day return in great power and glory as their Judge (Matt. 25:31).
2. When Jesus rules in glory, all humankind will have to account for their actions (vss. 32-33).
3. The upright demonstrate their love for the Lord by serving others in need (vss. 34-36).
4. Jesus is fully aware of our acts of kindness and compassion toward others (vss. 37-40).
5. During the Saviour's glorious reign, the wicked will be consigned to the place of eternal torment (vs. 41).
6. The unrighteous, despite their claims, will not be able to prove to the Redeemer that they reached out to others in need (vss. 42-45).
7. Christ holds all people responsible for what they think, say, and do in this life (vs. 46).

—*Dan Lioy.*

FOR DAILY MEDITATION

MONDAY, July 17.   Dan. 7:9-14.

Authority given to the Son of Man. Jesus frequently referred to Himself as the "Son of Man," which is a title drawn from Daniel's prophetic vision. He is uniquely qualified and found worthy to approach the overwhelming holiness of God the Father, wherein He is commissioned to reign with authority and execute judgment on behalf of the Ancient of Days. We look forward to our risen Saviour reigning in perfect righteousness.

TUESDAY, July 18.   Matt. 16:24-28.

A coming judgment. Jesus has ascended back to His Father in heaven, but He has promised to return. What went unnoticed by so many during His earthly ministry, due to the hardness of and unbelief in their hearts, will become undeniable. Jesus will return in the glory of God the Father, and those who rejected Him and His gift of salvation will not be able to escape judgment.

WEDNESDAY, July 19.   Ps. 9:1-10.

Judging the world in righteousness. The Lord is the Most High God, and He rules over all nations and their so-called gods. He sees all that transpires in the world and is there to help us whenever trouble arises. Unrighteousness opposes His holiness and is temporarily allowed to exist because of the Lord's patience and mercy. But all unrighteousness will be judged and done away with forever when the Lord reigns in His righteousness.

THURSDAY, July 20. Jas. 2:14-20.

Evidence of faith. What you believe can be articulated and expressed to others with words, but you cannot show it to them apart from your actions. Merely claiming to trust and belong to the Lord can be done by anyone. The genuineness of your faith, however, will either be proven real or fake in the eyes of world based on how you live your life and respond to adversity. What kind of faith are you showing the world?

FRIDAY, July 21.   Jas. 1:22-27.

Pure religion. The inward motivation behind our outward actions remains hidden from other people, but God sees and knows all. The widows and orphans among James's original audience would have lacked riches to repay others for their acts of kindness. Believers were not to be deterred from loving and helping the least among them on the basis of their inability to repay. The desire to glorify God when helping others ensures that our service is pure.

SATURDAY, July 22.   II Thess. 1:3-10.

God judges rightly. Suffering to one extent or another is an inescapable reality experienced by God's people. Even though we would rather do without affliction, we should be encouraged to know that God is with us to sustain us through our suffering. He is also working through our situations to draw us closer to Himself and to make us more like Jesus. Those who target God's people for persecution will not escape His justice.

SUNDAY, July 23.   Matt. 25:31-46.

Judgment of the nations. Israel's Messiah is the Saviour of the entire world—of as many as will put their faith in Him to save them. Jesus will render the final judgment for all people of every nation, Jews and Gentiles. Faith in Jesus as Saviour marks one's status as one of His sheep. Pray now that God would work in the hearts of people of all nations to help them recognize Jesus as the Good Shepherd who laid down and took His life back up for them.

—*Reginald Coats.*

LESSON 9　　　　　　　　　　　　　　　　　　　　　　　　　　JULY 30, 2023

Scripture Lesson Text

MATT. 13:9 Who hath ears to hear, let him hear.

10 And the disciples came, and said unto him, Why speakest thou unto them in parables?

11 He answered and said unto them, Because it is given unto you to know the mysteries of the kingdom of heaven, but to them it is not given.

12 For whosoever hath, to him shall be given, and he shall have more abundance: but whosoever hath not, from him shall be taken away even that he hath.

13 Therefore speak I to them in parables: because they seeing see not; and hearing they hear not, neither do they understand.

14 And in them is fulfilled the prophecy of Esaias, which saith, By hearing ye shall hear, and shall not understand; and seeing ye shall see, and shall not perceive:

15 For this people's heart is waxed gross, and *their* ears are dull of hearing, and their eyes they have closed; lest at any time they should see with *their* eyes, and hear with *their* ears, and should understand with *their* heart, and should be converted, and I should heal them.

16 But blessed *are* your eyes, for they see: and your ears, for they hear.

17 For verily I say unto you, That many prophets and righteous *men* have desired to see *those things* which ye see, and have not seen *them;* and to hear *those things* which ye hear, and have not heard *them.*

NOTES

Ears to Hear

Lesson Text: Matthew 13:9-17

Related Scriptures: Matthew 13:18-23; I Corinthians 2:6-16

TIME: A.D. 28   PLACE: Sea of Galilee

GOLDEN TEXT—"Who hath ears to hear, let him hear" (Matthew 13:9).

Lesson Exposition

The parable of the sower forms the backdrop of Jesus' statement in Matthew 13:9. As Jesus sat by the seaside, a multitude of people gathered to hear Him teach. He told the story of a man who went out to plant seeds in a field. Although the farmer in Jesus' story planted his seeds lavishly, the different kinds of ground where the seeds fell determined how the plants would grow.

JESUS' EXHORTATION—Matt. 13:9

The parable of the sower lists four outcomes—three in which people do not remain committed and one in which a person does. The last category is those who hear, believe, and act on God's Word. These are the ones Jesus was talking about in Matthew 13:9. Their openness and willingness to obey the commandments of Christ bring blessings into their lives and make them a blessing to others. To different degrees, their good deeds bear much fruit for the kingdom (vs. 23). In addition, the fruit they bear will be a blessing for themselves as well.

When we hear and receive God's Word, faith comes alive in our hearts. The Spirit convicts us of our sins and comes to dwell in us so that we can live godly lives. As a result, we are increasingly transformed into the image of Christ. Spiritual growth continues as we regularly pray, read the Bible, and fellowship with other believers.

God calls us to be not only hearers but also doers of His Word (Jas. 1:22). Jesus told His disciples that they were to be like salt that seasons and light that gives the brightness of God's love to the world (Matt. 5:13-16). God uses us to work His divine purpose here on earth.

JESUS' EXPLANATION—Matt. 13:10-17

The question asked by the disciples (Matt. 13:10). After Jesus finished presenting the parable of the sower, He separated somewhat from the multitudes. Perhaps He was back in the house where He had started the day and to which He retreated (vs. 36). Taking advantage of a moment of privacy, His disciples asked why He favored telling stories to people instead of simply stating the facts.

Jesus' parables usually emphasized one primary concept that could be applied in a variety of ways. Not all the details of a parable necessarily had significance. (This serves as a caution against reading too much into a parable.) The parables motivated interested listeners (such as the disciples) to find out more about what was being taught. At the same time, the parables hid the truth from disinterested listeners (such as proud religious leaders).

It may be that the disciples did not realize that the spiritual truths Jesus was relating were incomprehensible to the ungodly. In addition, they may not have realized that the majority of listeners in the multitudes were to be counted among those who could not hear the truth with understanding.

The fulfillment of prophecy (Matt. 13:11-15). In these verses, we discover that those who want to do God's will must understand the principles of His kingdom. It was necessary, then, that Jesus speak with the greatest clarity. That is why He made extensive use of parables, such as the one about a farmer sowing seed.

Jesus used parables because He wanted to make the truth understandable to those who were ready to learn, but He had another reason for using this method of instruction. It gave His followers an understanding of the kingdom's mysteries (information not previously revealed). At the same time, those who were not following Him were left in the dark. Those who were open to the Saviour's teaching would receive more understanding; in contrast, those who refused to heed His words would eventually forfeit what little spiritual insight they had.

Christ noted that the prophecy recorded in Isaiah 6:9-10 found its ultimate fulfillment in those who spurned His teaching. Though the religious leaders of His day (as in Isaiah's day) heard what Jesus declared, they failed to appropriate His truths to their lives. In brief, their spiritually hardened condition prevented them from turning to Jesus in faith for spiritual healing.

The pronouncement of blessing (Matt. 13:16-17). Jesus declared that His followers were the objects of God's love and favor. He showered them with eternal blessings, for they chose to respond in faith and obedience to the Saviour's teachings. In fact, their clear grasp of eternal truths eclipsed what the Old Testament prophets and other godly forebears had understood. They had longed to see and hear what Jesus' followers were privileged to know about the divine kingdom. May our attitude likewise reflect a longing to know Christ.

—*Dan Lioy.*

PRACTICAL POINTS

1. The Lord wants us to heed the truth of His Word in every area of our lives (Matt. 13:9).
2. When we are perplexed about the things of God, we can trust Jesus to guide us into a clearer understanding of the truth (vs. 10).
3. It is an eternal privilege and blessing for us to be able to grasp truths associated with the divine kingdom (vs. 11).
4. Those who in their ignorance and unbelief spurn the things of God remain blinded to the truth of His Word (vss. 12-15).
5. Through His Spirit, the Lord enables us to respond in a constructive way to the mysteries of the kingdom that have been revealed through Scripture (vs. 16).
6. We often fail to appreciate how privileged we are to be the recipients of the truths that Jesus taught (vs. 17).

—*Dan Lioy.*

FOR DAILY MEDITATION

MONDAY, July 24.   Ps. 78:1-8.
Listen to my instruction. Failing to remember God's instructions and wonderful blessings leads down a dangerous path. The people of Israel made that mistake on numerous occasions, and the consequences were never good. The call to remember and follow the ways of the Lord was not only for the present generation of Israelites but was also to be passed on to their children. Are you careful to remember His goodness and tell others about the benefits of following His ways?

TUESDAY, July 25.   Matt. 13:18-23.
Receiving God's Word. You might receive numerous gifts over the course of your life. Some of them may be more precious to you than others. The value of God's Word is beyond measure whether the recipients of it recognize its worth or not. Through the pages of Scripture, we learn what our awesome God desires to make known of Himself and His will to us. In what ways have you noticed God's Word taking root in your life?

WEDNESDAY, July 26.   Isa. 6:8-12.
Hearing without understanding. If someone is speaking to you while your mind is preoccupied with other matters, you might fail to understand what is being said. The people of Israel remained preoccupied with their own desires even as God repeatedly sent messages to them via His prophets. Their failure to hear, understand, and respond to the Lord was eventually met with chastisement. God is patient, but we should respond to His Word with urgency.

THURSDAY, July 27.   Rom. 16:25-27.
Revealed mystery of Christ. A masterful plan can take years to come together. The *most* masterful plan of all time actually predates human history and was already in place before the creation of the world. The precise manner in which God would bring His gift of salvation to the world was previously hidden but culminated and revealed for both Jews and Gentiles with the death, burial, and resurrection of Jesus Christ.

FRIDAY, July 28.   I Cor. 2:6-16.
Taught by the Spirit. All that the world can offer is nothing in comparison to the hope and promises that God gives His people through His Word. As we study Scripture, the Holy Spirit encourages us and helps us to better understand the glorious future that God has in store for us. Unbelievers discard the deep riches of Scripture, but we can still treasure them for what they actually are.

SATURDAY, July 29.   I Pet. 1:22-25.
Imperishable seed. Along with His gift of salvation, God imparts His Spirit and a new nature in us when we trust Jesus as Saviour. As Christians, the love of God should be evident in our lives. Loving others in light of how God has loved and continues to love us bears witness to us being His children. God's Word, Spirit, and love are working to transform our lives for the sake of His glory.

SUNDAY, July 30.   Matt. 13:9-17.
Hearing God's Word. There is a distinction between merely hearing God's Word and actually being receptive to it. Those who heard Jesus' teaching also needed to gain understanding and apply the truth received from Him to their lives. God is pleased when we have a desire to hear from Him and a willingness to respond in faith to what He has said. As you study the Bible, pray that God would help you to better understand His Word.

—Reginald Coats.

LESSON 10   AUGUST 6, 2023

Scripture Lesson Text

MATT. 18:21 Then came Peter to him, and said, Lord, how oft shall my brother sin against me, and I forgive him? till seven times?

22 Jesus saith unto him, I say not unto thee, Until seven times: but, Until seventy times seven.

23 Therefore is the kingdom of heaven likened unto a certain king, which would take account of his servants.

24 And when he had begun to reckon, one was brought unto him, which owed him ten thousand talents.

25 But forasmuch as he had not to pay, his lord commanded him to be sold, and his wife, and children, and all that he had, and payment to be made.

26 The servant therefore fell down, and worshipped him, saying, Lord, have patience with me, and I will pay thee all.

27 Then the lord of that servant was moved with compassion, and loosed him, and forgave him the debt.

28 But the same servant went out, and found one of his fellowservants, which owed him an hundred pence: and he laid hands on him, and took *him* **by the throat, saying, Pay me that thou owest.**

29 And his fellowservant fell down at his feet, and besought him, saying, Have patience with me, and I will pay thee all.

30 And he would not: but went and cast him into prison, till he should pay the debt.

31 So when his fellowservants saw what was done, they were very sorry, and came and told unto their lord all that was done.

32 Then his lord, after that he had called him, said unto him, O thou wicked servant, I forgave thee all that debt, because thou desiredst me:

33 Shouldest not thou also have had compassion on thy fellowservant, even as I had pity on thee?

34 And his lord was wroth, and delivered him to the tormentors, till he should pay all that was due unto him.

35 So likewise shall my heavenly Father do also unto you, if ye from your hearts forgive not every one his brother their trespasses.

NOTES

Forgiving One Another

Lesson Text: Matthew 18:21-35

Related Scriptures: Luke 6:27-38; 17:1-4

TIME: A.D. 29   PLACE: Capernaum

GOLDEN TEXT—"Then his lord, after that he had called him, said unto him, O thou wicked servant, I forgave thee all that debt, because thou desiredst me: shouldest not thou also have had compassion on thy fellowservant, even as I had pity on thee?" (Matthew 18:32-33).

Lesson Exposition

Peter probably expected Jesus to praise him for being so magnanimous when he asked about forgiving a person seven times. Instead, Jesus taught that a spirit of forgiveness is unlimited. Our model, the forgiving Lord who suffered on the cross, meant that we should never tally the number of times we extend mercy. The arithmetic of love never keeps score.

A KING'S PITY—Matt. 18:21-27

Unlimited forgiveness stressed (Matt. 18:21-22). As Jesus instructed the disciples about disciplining and forgiving fellow believers, Peter raised a question. He wondered whether forgiving an offender up to seven times was sufficient. Peter had been generous in his estimate. The rabbis generally taught that forgiveness should be limited to three times. Peter had more than doubled that stipulation.

If Peter, and the others, wanted to put a limit on forgiveness, Jesus gave them one. His answer must have stunned them. Forgiving someone seven times would not be enough, even though that number surpassed the old rules. No, it would have to be seventy times seven. Seven was the number of perfection with the Jews, so Jesus was using that concept to show that forgiveness is endless, ever-renewing, and continuing forever. In other words, we cannot put limits on our forgiveness.

Unlimited forgiveness illustrated (Matt. 18:23-27). Jesus told a parable in which a king, in the course of an audit, decided to collect his outstanding debts. There was one subject who owed the king an enormous amount, namely, ten thousand talents. The servant, no doubt a high-ranking government official, was unable to pay off his debt. Since executing the man would yield nothing, the king ordered him, his family, and his possessions to be seized and sold. A partial payment was better than nothing.

The panicked servant pleaded for mercy, promising that he would repay the king. Of course, his promise was absurd. The king, however, was moved by the man's request and agreed to forgive the debt.

A SERVANT'S REVENGE—Matt. 18:28-35

The servant's spiteful response (Matt. 18:28-34). The servant left the king's palace and immediately found a fellow servant who was indebted to him. The first servant grabbed the other man by his throat and began demanding payment for a relatively modest amount of money. Nearly choking, the second servant gasped out the same request for mercy that the first servant had used.

In Jesus' parable, the first servant refused to be merciful in spite of having received mercy himself. He had the poor servant thrown into debtors' prison, where he would remain until the debt was satisfied. A tightly knit cluster of royal servants were outraged by the injustice; so as a group they spoke with the king.

The king was furious. He summoned the first servant and angrily lectured him on the matter of forgiveness. The monarch called the servant "wicked" (vs. 32) and censured him for not being as merciful to a fellow servant as the king had been to him. Then the irate ruler ordered the servant to be imprisoned and tortured until his entire debt was repaid.

The Saviour's warning (Matt. 18:35). The ungrateful servant should have treated others as he himself had been treated. In His application, the Saviour pointed out that this is also what God expects of those who have experienced His forgiveness. Jesus' words also imply that God will similarly treat those who refuse to forgive. They will be shown the same measure of mercy that they have extended to others.

When we stand in judgment against others, no matter how just our cause seems to us, in effect we are discounting the great mercy Christ has shown to us. How can we say that another person's offense against us is even comparable to our offense against God?

Of course, we know that it takes divine empowerment for us to truly forgive people for some of the worst wrongs done to us. We therefore must always seek God's help as we try to rise above our weakness of character, our anger and self-pity, and our desire to hate and find some way to pay back evil for evil.

We also need divine assistance in order to let go of those feelings of rage and resentment and instead pay back evil with good while trusting in God's ability to carry out justice. When we forgive as Christ has taught us, we become a special people—a blessing to God and to others, as well as to ourselves.

—Dan Lioy.

PRACTICAL POINTS

1. Often we underestimate the extent to which God wants us to be forgiving to others (Matt. 18:21).
2. God's understanding of what it means to truly forgive others far exceeds what we could ever have anticipated (vs. 22).
3. There are experiences in the temporal world that serve to illustrate eternal heavenly truths (vs. 23).
4. When we encounter the holiness and justice of God, we are grateful for His mercy extended to us in Christ (vss. 24-27).
5. God is displeased when we, as forgiven sinners, do not respond with unconditional mercy to others who have offended us (vss. 28-30).
6. Our Lord is serious about the need to be compassionate and forgiving toward our fellow human beings (vss. 31-34).
7. The prospect of judgment is a strong incentive to forgive (vs. 35).

—Dan Lioy.

FOR DAILY MEDITATION

MONDAY, July 31.   Luke 6:27-38.
Love and forgive enemies. Any time you show love to someone, you are imitating God. Loving those who treat you kindly might not seem all that challenging, but Jesus taught that His followers are also to love their enemies. Our natural inclination is to repay and treat people according to how they have treated us. But what if God did the same when dealing with us? God's love and forgiveness were extended to us through Christ, and we should follow His perfect example.

TUESDAY, Aug. 1.   Luke 7:36-50.
Much love with much forgiveness. Failing to recognize one's own sins can lead to viewing others in a condescending way. No one is beyond being rescued by Jesus and His love. And likewise, no one is beyond needing His forgiveness. Whether we see ourselves as the most offensive of sinners or as the least, we are helpless and hopeless apart from God's love and forgiveness. We should, therefore, make a point of loving and forgiving others as God loves and has forgiven us.

WEDNESDAY, Aug. 2.   Ps. 78:32-40.
Mercy to the unfaithful. As the psalmist looked back over the course of Israel's history, he could not help seeing the Lord's mercy at work time and time again. If we were to look back over the course of our lives, we would also see the persistence of God's mercy. In our times of disobedience and unfaithfulness to God, He has never stopped loving us. Praise Him for showing mercy to the unfaithful!

THURSDAY, Aug. 3. Col. 3:12-17.
Called to forgive. You should have a good reason for making the choices that you make. As Christians, we have a great reason to forgive others; God has forgiven us. Being the recipients of God's forgiveness is cause for us to extend forgiveness to those who have offended us. If deserving forgiveness were prerequisite to receiving it, we would all still be separated from God and dead in our trespasses and sins.

FRIDAY, Aug. 4.   Luke 17:3-4.
Always willing to forgive. Bad habits can be hard to break, and good habits can seem difficult to maintain. Nevertheless, Jesus calls for His followers to be diligent when it comes to forgiving others. Having a willingness to forgive is extremely important as believers in Christ and members of God's family. The way that we love and forgive one another is an example to the world of our Heavenly Father's love and forgiveness.

SATURDAY, Aug. 5.   Eph. 1:3-10.
Forgiveness through the blood. We receive God's forgiveness for all our sins through faith in Jesus Christ and what He accomplished for us with His death and resurrection. He suffered the Father's wrath against sin on our behalf, and His life is the price that was paid so that we could justly be forgiven. Praise God for the forgiveness found in His Son, Jesus!

SUNDAY, Aug. 6.   Matt. 18:21-35.
Repeated forgiveness. Holding grudges and treating people harshly after being offended is devoid of mercy and forgiveness. However, God does not withhold mercy or forgiveness when dealing with us. In spite of how many times someone might sin against us, we have sinned against God more. And no matter how much forgiveness we might extend to an offender, God's forgiveness has been bestowed upon us to a much greater extent. Is there someone whom you need to forgive right now?
—*Reginald Coats.*

LESSON 11   AUGUST 13, 2023

SCRIPTURE LESSON TEXT

LUKE 15:11 And he said, A certain man had two sons:

12 And the younger of them said to *his* father, Father, give me the portion of goods that falleth *to me*. And he divided unto them *his* living.

13 And not many days after the younger son gathered all together, and took his journey into a far country, and there wasted his substance with riotous living.

14 And when he had spent all, there arose a mighty famine in that land; and he began to be in want.

15 And he went and joined himself to a citizen of that country; and he sent him into his fields to feed swine.

16 And he would fain have filled his belly with the husks that the swine did eat: and no man gave unto him.

17 And when he came to himself, he said, How many hired servants of my father's have bread enough and to spare, and I perish with hunger!

18 I will arise and go to my father, and will say unto him, Father, I have sinned against heaven, and before thee,

19 And am no more worthy to be called thy son: make me as one of thy hired servants.

20 And he arose, and came to his father. But when he was yet a great way off, his father saw him, and had compassion, and ran, and fell on his neck, and kissed him.

21 And the son said unto him, Father, I have sinned against heaven, and in thy sight, and am no more worthy to be called thy son.

22 But the father said to his servants, Bring forth the best robe, and put *it* on him; and put a ring on his hand, and shoes on *his* feet:

23 And bring hither the fatted calf, and kill *it*; and let us eat, and be merry:

24 For this my son was dead, and is alive again; he was lost, and is found. And they began to be merry.

NOTES

A Story of Forgiveness

Lesson Text: Luke 15:11-24

Related Scriptures: Luke 15:25-32; Romans 12:9-21; II Corinthians 5:17-21

TIME: A.D. 30   PLACE: probably Perea

GOLDEN TEXT—"This my son was dead, and is alive again; he was lost, and is found" (Luke 15:24).

Lesson Exposition

The story of the prodigal son is perhaps the best known of all Jesus' parables. The two parables that precede it likewise focus on something lost being found (Luke 15:3-10). The lesson is that God seeks and welcomes repentant sinners; He does not despise and ignore them as the scribes and the Pharisees did (vss. 1-2). The parable of the lost son reiterates this point and more directly addresses the issue of repentance (cf. vss. 7, 10) (Michaels, *Servant and Son,* John Knox).

THE SON'S REQUEST—
Luke 15:11-12

Jesus began His story by introducing a man and his two sons. The older son is not mentioned again until verse 25, and while he has an important role in the story, he is not the focus of our study.

The younger son approached his father and asked for his inheritance. Normally, this was received upon the death of the father, but it could be requested before the father died. It becomes clear, however, that the request here reflected the selfish and foolish attitude of the son. Still, his father granted his request.

THE SON'S DESPERATION—
Luke 15:13-16

Riotous living (Luke 15:13-14). In Jesus' story, the son took his inheritance and left for a "far country." There he quickly squandered all he had "with riotous living." The idea is that he lived recklessly, wasting his money with no thought of tomorrow.

Because of his foolish wastefulness, the man had no resources to fall back on when a famine arose in the land (vs. 14). As a result, he began to be "in want."

Ruinous results (Luke 15:15-16). Without money for food, and with no one to help him, the son took the only job he could find—feeding pigs. The picture Jesus painted was one of utter degradation for a Jewish person—working for a Gentile and feeding unclean animals. Indeed, the son even longed for the food he fed the pigs.

THE SON'S DECISION—
Luke 15:17-19

His realization (Luke 15:17). In his despair, the son's thoughts turned to what he had left behind. Even his father's servants had plenty to eat, yet he was starving. Sometimes it takes hardship to bring a person to his senses.

His repentance (Luke 15:18-19). The son determined to return home, confess his sin—which he rightly saw as "against heaven"—and humbly ask, not to be a son again, but to be one of his father's hired servants. While the son was initially motivated to return home because of his circumstances, his words reflect a humble, repentant attitude that expected nothing more from his father than a servant would expect.

THE SON'S RETURN—
Luke 15:20-24

His father's greeting (Luke 15:20-21). When the son returned home, his father saw him approaching and had "compassion" on him. He was moved inwardly with pity and love, and he expressed it immediately by running to his son and embracing and kissing him.

It is evident that the father in Jesus' parable is symbolic of God. God has infinite compassion for sinners and eagerly accepts all who repent and trust in Him.

The father soon experienced his son's repentance. The very fact that he had come home would likely point to a repentant attitude. However, the son proceeded to offer the heartfelt speech he had rehearsed.

His father's rejoicing (Luke 15:22-24). The father wasted no time in calling for his servants to bring the best clothing for his son and to prepare a great feast to celebrate his return. There was no thought of punishing him or making him a hired servant. He was his son, and he would be treated accordingly. He had been lost, but now he was found. He had been assumed physically dead, but now he was alive.

Indeed, the portrait Jesus presented was of one who had been spiritually dead but now was alive because he had repented and come to God in faith. Only repentance and faith can reconcile lost sinners with the holy God.

Sometimes people must reap the consequences of their own foolishness before they can clearly see God's grace, but no one is beyond the reach of God's love and mercy. This is the lesson the Jewish leaders needed to learn, and the lesson we need to learn as well.

God rejoices over the repentance of every sinner. Let us not give up on anyone or stand in the way of someone coming to Christ. Let us be patient, consistent witnesses to the unsaved around us so that we might rejoice with God and the angels when they repent.

—Jarl K. Waggoner.

PRACTICAL POINTS

1. One who lives only for today with no plans for tomorrow is a fool who will regret his actions (Luke 15:11-13).
2. A person who thinks only of himself usually ends up suffering by himself with no one to help him (vss. 14-15).
3. Hardship is often the means God uses to bring sinners to their senses (vss. 16-17).
4. All sin is against God and must be confessed to Him (vss. 18-19).
5. Rather than abandon those who have strayed from God, we should have compassion on them (vss. 20-21).
6. We should reflect the grace of our God by faithfully loving others and joyously receiving all who repent, even as God receives them (vss. 22-24).

—Jarl K. Waggoner.

Home Study

FOR DAILY MEDITATION

MONDAY, Aug. 7.   Deut. 21:15-17.
Firstborn's portion. In many ancient Near Eastern cultures, a man's firstborn son was thought to signify his father's masculinity. The cultural norm was that a firstborn son would inherit a double portion of his father's wealth as he became the family's patriarch. While God never prescribed or condoned polygamous relationships, He gave instructions to His people to ensure that, within such familial situations, a father could not bypass bestowing the firstborn inheritance to a son on the basis of favoring one wife over another.

TUESDAY, Aug. 8.   Matt. 7:7-12.
Grace of the Father. All of God's goodness toward us is completely undeserved, and yet He delights in bestowing it upon us. Through faith in Jesus as Saviour, we were spiritually brought back to life and into a relationship with God as His children. We can now bring our praise and petitions before Him in prayer. Persistence in prayer is one way that we can express our reliance and hope in our awesome God.

WEDNESDAY, Aug. 9.   Ps. 86:1-7.
Prayer for mercy. When in need, David always remembered that he could turn to the Lord for help. By calling on the Lord, he was confident that there would always be a sufficient amount of mercy to sustain him through his struggles. A habit of relying on the Lord is a recipe for having peace even when faced with overwhelming problems.

THURSDAY, Aug. 10.   Ezek. 18:21-23.
Turn from sin and live. As soon as you realize that you are heading in the wrong direction, you should change your course. People who have made mistakes and bad decisions do not have to continue in the error of their ways. Because of God's mercy, even the wicked have an opportunity to turn to Him and find forgiveness. Instead of remaining separated from Him because of sin, God's desire is for people to turn to Him and live. Praise God that we can turn to Him and receive the gift of eternal life through faith in Jesus Christ!

FRIDAY, Aug. 11.   Luke 15:25-32.
Welcome the repentant. Many people like taking vacations and getting away for a while, but returning home can also be a joyous occasion. The greatest amount of joy in Jesus' parable was experienced by the father upon the return of his youngest son. Even though he had previously made a decision that greatly dishonored his father and family, the son came to his senses and returned home. God rejoices and welcomes into His family everyone who trusts Jesus as Saviour.

SATURDAY, Aug. 12.   Isa. 57:15-21.
God will comfort the repentant. Even when God disciplines His people, hope can be found in Him. Correcting is an expression of God's love for His people. Because God cares, He is involved in our lives and is there to comfort us even when we have brought pain and suffering upon ourselves. Take strength in knowing that God's comfort is never more than a prayer away.

SUNDAY, Aug. 13.   Luke 15:11-24.
Repentance and reconciliation. Repentance on the part of the younger son in Jesus' parable was expressed not only through his return home but also through his admitting that he had sinned and willing to be treated by his father as a servant. The father's love and willingness to forgive is what empowers reconciliation in the parable just as God extends reconciliation to us through His Son, Jesus Christ.
—*Reginald Coats.*

LESSON 12   AUGUST 20, 2023

Scripture Lesson Text

MATT. 20:1 For the kingdom of heaven is like unto a man *that is* an householder, which went out early in the morning to hire labourers into his vineyard.

2 And when he had agreed with the labourers for a penny a day, he sent them into his vineyard.

3 And he went out about the third hour, and saw others standing idle in the marketplace,

4 And said unto them; Go ye also into the vineyard, and whatsoever is right I will give you. And they went their way.

5 Again he went out about the sixth and ninth hour, and did likewise.

6 And about the eleventh hour he went out, and found others standing idle, and saith unto them, Why stand ye here all the day idle?

7 They say unto him, Because no man hath hired us. He saith unto them, Go ye also into the vineyard; and whatsoever is right, *that* shall ye receive.

8 So when even was come, the lord of the vineyard saith unto his steward, Call the labourers, and give them *their* hire, beginning from the last unto the first.

9 And when they came that *were hired* about the eleventh hour, they received every man a penny.

10 But when the first came, they supposed that they should have received more; and they likewise received every man a penny.

11 And when they had received *it,* they murmured against the goodman of the house,

12 Saying, These last have wrought *but* one hour, and thou hast made them equal unto us, which have borne the burden and heat of the day.

13 But he answered one of them, and said, Friend, I do thee no wrong: didst not thou agree with me for a penny?

14 Take *that* thine *is,* and go thy way: I will give unto this last, even as unto thee.

15 Is it not lawful for me to do what I will with mine own? Is thine eye evil, because I am good?

16 So the last shall be first, and the first last: for many be called, but few chosen.

NOTES

Home Study   55

God's Gracious Rewards

Lesson Text: Matthew 20:1-16

Related Scriptures: Matthew 19:16-30; 20:20-28; Luke 13:22-30

TIME: A.D. 30   PLACE: Perea

GOLDEN TEXT—"[The man] said unto them; Go ye also into the vineyard, and whatsoever is right I will give you. And they went their way" (Matthew 20:4).

Lesson Exposition

In order to understand the parable in this week's lesson, one note of cultural history must be brought to light. In Jesus' day, as well as in Old Testament times, laborers worked on a day-to-day basis. They presented themselves in the town marketplace when they were available for work. At the end of the day's work, they were paid for that day's labor.

This was an Old Testament principle (Lev. 19:13; Deut. 24:15). If a laborer did not work, he would not be paid for the day. He and his family would not have money for meeting essential needs; thus, daily work and daily pay were crucial to those who labored in farms and vineyards.

HIRING THE LABORERS—
Matt. 20:1-7

A kingdom parable (Matt. 20:1). The parable of this lesson gives added information to answer Peter's question in 19:27. The "for" (20:1) reveals a continuation of the thought of 19:30 (cf. 20:16). Emphasis is on the fact that as a householder faithfully pays his workers in a gracious manner, so rewards in the kingdom will be graciously distributed by the One dispensing the rewards. Those who serve Christ the longest may not receive the greatest rewards.

Hiring in the morning (Matt. 20:2-4). The vineyard owner hired men in the early morning and offered to pay them a denarius, the normal wage for a day's work. At the "third hour" (9:00 A.M.), he returned to the marketplace and saw more men who needed work; so he hired them and promised them a fair wage.

Hiring in the afternoon (Matt. 20:5). The vineyard owner returned to the marketplace at the sixth hour (noon) and the ninth hour (3:00 P.M.). Again he hired men who needed work and sent them to work in his vineyard.

Hiring near quitting time (Matt. 20:6-7). Once again, the vineyard owner went to the marketplace. It was now "the eleventh hour" (5:00 P.M.), and there were still men needing work. When they lamented to the vineyard owner that the day was almost over and they had received no work and thus would receive no pay, they were immediately hired and sent to the vineyard. They were promised fair compensation for their labors.

PAYING THE LABORERS—
Matt. 20:8-12

Receiving their pay (Matt. 20:8-9). When the day's work was done, the paymaster was told to pay the laborers. The first to be paid were those who had been hired near quitting time. They received a full day's pay.

Reviling their patron (Matt. 20:10-12). The workers who had been hired in the early morning had seen that the latecomers had been paid a denarius; so they expected to be paid additional to the denarius they had been promised; but they were paid the same wage. They were not happy and began to grumble about the fairness of the vineyard owner. Although they had worked through the heat of the day, they had been paid the same as those who had worked only an hour.

LOVING THE LABORERS—
Matt. 20:13-16

An agreement honored (Matt. 20:13-14). The vineyard owner reminded one of the complainers that he had been paid exactly what had been agreed upon when he was hired. The vineyard owner then expressed his desire to do good for those who had been hired late in the day. He would pay them the same as the others, not because they had worked an equal amount of time, but because they had equal needs.

A need met (Matt. 20:15-16). The vineyard owner was not trying to cheat anyone; rather, he was trying to show mercy. He had the right to give more than expected to some if he desired. The first-hired laborers were not to be envious of his generosity.

"It is frightening to realize that our identification with the first workers, and hence with the opponents of Jesus, reveals how loveless and unmerciful we basically are. We may be more 'under law' in our thinking and less 'under grace' than we realize. God is good and compassionate far beyond his children's understanding" (Stein, *An Introduction to the Parables of Jesus,* Westminster).

Jesus ended the parable with a foundational truth of God's kingdom. God deals with people as He wills, not as people sense fairness (vs. 16).

God is interested in meeting our needs. He wants everyone to be saved (II Pet. 3:9). His mercy and grace are extended to all people because of their need. As giving a day's wage to those who did not earn it was an act of grace, so giving salvation, certainly undeserved, to sinful mankind is God's ultimate act of grace!

—Terry Clark.

PRACTICAL POINTS

1. God is eager to give us opportunities to labor for the sake of His kingdom (Matt. 20:1-2).
2. It is important to offer a person appropriate compensation for his labors (vss. 3-4).
3. Idleness creates want, and God does not want us to be in want (vss. 5-6).
4. We may expect fairness in our relationship with God, but God's understanding and insight far exceeds our own (vss. 7-9).
5. When an employer has kept his word, he should not be maligned by his employees (vss. 10-12).
6. We should never complain when God's goodness is extended to someone we might judge unworthy (vss. 13-15).
7. God's judgments are often very different from ours (vs. 16).

—Terry Clark.

FOR DAILY MEDITATION

MONDAY, Aug. 14. Matt. 19:16-22.

A rich man's sorrow. There are some things that are humanly impossible. Being able to obtain eternal life with one's own efforts fits into that category. The question posed to Jesus by the rich man, however, indicates that he believed otherwise. His departure in sorrow actually exposed the truth of the matter: he loved his riches more than God. He needed to be delivered from sin just as we all do.

TUESDAY, Aug. 15. Matt. 19:23-30.

Salvation only by God's grace. Having wealth was believed to be a sign of God's favor, and if a rich person could only enter God's kingdom with great difficulty, the feat would have seemed impossible for anyone else. More than just *seeming* like an impossibility, no one can enter heaven apart from having faith in the Lord to do so. Only by God's grace can anyone be saved.

WEDNESDAY, Aug. 16. Jas. 3:13-18.

Beware of envy. Being envious of someone is an indication of not being content with one's own situation. Our faith in Jesus does not make everything go exactly the way that we might desire, but we should remain confident in trusting that the Lord loves us and is working in and through each of our lives for His glory. We should be thankful for all that the Lord has and has not blessed us with.

THURSDAY, Aug. 17. Luke 13:22-30.

The last will be first. How would you like to be first in line only to later discover that what you believed to be the start of the line was actually the end? You would experience surprise and disappointment once you realized the truth. A similar reaction but to a much greater detriment will be realized by all who have tried to achieve salvation by any means other than trusting Jesus. Rejoice that you know God through faith in His Son, Jesus.

FRIDAY, Aug. 18. Matt. 20:20-23.

God will assign us our place. In the moments leading up to His crucifixion, Jesus again told His disciples what awaited Him upon arriving in Jerusalem. The disciples, however, continued to display a lack of understanding and instead of focusing on Jesus' words, they focused on themselves. As we serve the Lord, our focus should be on glorifying Him. He has prepared a special place for each of us.

SATURDAY, Aug. 19. Matt. 17:24-27.

Not demanding our privileges. Being the Son of God, Jesus should have been considered exempt from paying the tax in the temple—His Father's house. Nevertheless, He made provision for the temple tax to be paid on His behalf as well as that of Peter. Through faith in Jesus, we are brought into the family of God. Following our Saviour's example, we should not expect preferential treatment but opposition in the world. But God is with us through all that we face.

SUNDAY, Aug. 20. Matt. 20:1-16.

God's grace illustrated. All of the laborers in Jesus' parable were recipients of grace to one extent or another. The owner of the vineyard did not have to hire any of them. However, showing up to work at the end of the day and receiving a full day's wage meant that the owner was extremely gracious and generous to those laborers. At whatever point in life a person trusts Jesus as Saviour, we should be overjoyed for them receiving God's gracious gift of salvation.

—Reginald Coats.

LESSON 13 — AUGUST 27, 2023

Scripture Lesson Text

LUKE 18:9 And he spake this parable unto certain which trusted in themselves that they were righteous, and despised others:

10 Two men went up into the temple to pray; the one a Pharisee, and the other a publican.

11 The Pharisee stood and prayed thus with himself, God, I thank thee, that I am not as other men *are,* extortioners, unjust, adulterers, or even as this publican.

12 I fast twice in the week, I give tithes of all that I possess.

13 And the publican, standing afar off, would not lift up so much as *his* eyes unto heaven, but smote upon his breast, saying, God be merciful to me a sinner.

14 I tell you, this man went down to his house justified *rather* than the other: for every one that exalteth himself shall be abased; and he that humbleth himself shall be exalted.

NOTES

God's Great Mercy

Lesson Text: Luke 18:9-14

Related Scriptures: Matthew 18:1-5; 23:1-12;
Luke 16:14-17; Romans 3:10-30

TIME: A.D. 30   PLACE: on the way to Jerusalem

GOLDEN TEXT—"Every one that exalteth himself shall be abased; and he that humbleth himself shall be exalted" (Luke 18:14).

Lesson Exposition

One of the consistent complaints that Israel's religious elite had against Jesus was His social interaction with sinful people. Chief among these sinners were publicans, or tax collectors. Jesus, in fact, took a special interest in these despised people (cf. Luke 5:27-32; 15:1-2), and He would continue to do so as He approached the cross (cf. 19:1-10).

As His ministry drew toward the climax of the crucifixion and the resurrection, Jesus' conflicts with the scribes and the Pharisees intensified as He boldly addressed the error and pride of those religious leaders. He spoke directly to them and their need in the parable of Luke 18:9-14.

JESUS' INTRODUCTION—
Luke 18:9-10

Luke introduces Jesus' parable by explicitly stating that it was spoken to certain people who "trusted in themselves that they were righteous, and despised others" (vs. 9). It is clear from both the context (cf. 15:1-2; 16:14; 17:20) and the parable itself (18:10-12) that Jesus had in mind the Pharisees and the scribes.

While there were exceptions, these religious leaders typically were consumed with pride, believing they were more righteous than others because of their strict adherence to the various laws and customs of Judaism.

Jesus began His parable by introducing two characters who went to the temple to pray: a Pharisee and a publican (tax collector). The contrast could hardly have been greater. The Pharisees, arrogant and dismissive of those who did not meet their standard of righteousness, were nonetheless respected and admired as religious men who sought to honor God.

Tax collectors, on the other hand, were almost universally despised by their fellow Jews. They owed their jobs to Israel's Roman conquerors and collected taxes for them. This alone was enough to earn them the hatred of the Jewish people. But many of them also became wealthy by extorting exorbitant fees from their countrymen in the course of their work.

THE PHARISEE'S PRAYER—
Luke 18:11-12

Jesus described the Pharisee as offering a "prayer" that was self-congratulatory. He asked nothing of God, but he simply praised himself by thanking God that he was not like others—extortioners, evildoers, and adulterers. Such a claim would not be thought excessive, as typically a Pharisee would not be guilty of obvious external sins.

Jesus also portrayed the Pharisee as setting himself apart from the publican, saying he was not like "this publican" (vs. 11). "This" seems to be used in a derogatory manner (cf. 14:30; 15:2, 30). Such a spiteful attitude toward tax collectors certainly was the norm for the Pharisees.

Not only did the Pharisee pride himself on avoiding the sins of others, but he also faithfully practiced his religion. He fasted and gave tithes on everything he possessed, which meant going beyond what the law required.

The Pharisee was a model of legalistic righteousness. However, he failed to understand that "humility toward God and compassion for neighbor are the essence of true piety" (Stein, *Luke*, B&H); these traits he lacked. He saw no real need for God.

THE PUBLICAN'S PRAYER—
Luke 18:13

The publican's prayer was everything the Pharisee's was not. It was a humble, straightforward, and simple request directed to God: "Be merciful to me a sinner." He understood that he was a sinner who merited nothing from God but judgment. Even his posture expressed this. He compared himself to no one, but he acknowledged his sin and pleaded for God's mercy. "Merciful" speaks of propitiation by means of sacrifice. He was asking God to cover his sins so that divine wrath would be removed.

THE DIVINE PERSPECTIVE—
Luke 18:14

Jesus did not excuse sin, and He recognized publicans as among the worst of sinners (cf. Matt. 5:46-47); but He accepts all who repent of their sins. Even His disciple Levi (Matthew) had been a tax collector (Luke 5:27-28). The Pharisee's pride, however, would not allow him to admit his sin. Consequently, Jesus said he was not justified, or declared righteous, before God. Because the publican humbly admitted his sin and repented of it, he was given a righteous standing before God.

We must always keep in mind God's perspective. He exalts us only if we humbly acknowledge our need for Him. Pride is deadly. It destroys relationships, robs us of opportunities to help others, and keeps us from God.

—*Jarl K. Waggoner.*

PRACTICAL POINTS

1. When we have too high a view of ourselves, we naturally have too low a view of others (Luke 18:9).
2. The mere practice of prayer says little about a person; it is the quality of prayer that is important (vs. 10).
3. We do not impress God by comparing ourselves to other sinners (vs. 11).
4. Spiritual practices are good, but when we take pride in our performance of them, we rob them of all meaning (vs. 12).
5. The essence of godly humility is recognizing our unworthiness before God and simply seeking His mercy (vs. 13).
6. We sacrifice God's blessings in our lives when we insist on proudly exalting ourselves (vs. 14).

—*Jarl K. Waggoner.*

FOR DAILY MEDITATION

MONDAY, Aug. 21.   Rom. 3:21-26.
No place for boasting. Imagine trying to throw a ball to the moon. Despite your greatest effort, you would come up miserably short of achieving your objective. No matter how diligent people might be in trying to live right, they will likewise fall miserably short of living up to God's standard of righteousness, which is Himself. Praise God for crediting us with the righteousness of Christ when we turned to Him in faith!

TUESDAY, Aug. 22.   Matt. 6:16-18.
Fast in secret. While the Day of Atonement was the one day a year when the people of Israel had been instructed by the Lord to fast, in New Testament times there were weekly occasions in which some Pharisees and other Jews took up the practice. However, some made a point of being noticed and esteemed by others for their apparent piety when fasting. Jesus taught that such motives needed to be redirected in order to please God.

WEDNESDAY, Aug. 23.   Luke 16:13-15.
God knows the heart. A devout love for money and worldly possessions will certainly hinder us from being devoted servants of the Lord. Many of the Pharisees had a deep affection for money but wanted to appear righteous in the eyes of others. While they may have appeared righteous outwardly, God knew their inward desires. Our love for God should not be surpassed by anything.

THURSDAY, Aug. 24.   Matt. 23:1-12.
The proud humbled. Being addressed by esteemed titles catered to the prideful attitudes of many of the Jewish religious leaders. Jesus called attention to their deliberate attempts to attract praise for themselves. But those who exalt themselves will be humbled, and those who exalt the Lord will be exalted by Him. Only the Lord deserves the highest praise, and we praise Him for all of His goodness and mighty deeds.

FRIDAY, Aug. 25.   Matt. 18:1-5.
Faith like a child's. Losing sight of what the Lord deems to be important is a snare that we need to remain guarded against. Jesus' disciples were more concerned about their own prestige in God's kingdom instead of what their Saviour was about to endure in order to make them a part of it. Granted, their understanding was limited, but that was at least partially due to their thoughts being preoccupied with other matters. Instead of thinking big of themselves, they needed to focus on the Lord with the faith of child.

SATURDAY, Aug. 26.   Isa. 1:10-17.
Turn from false worship. Going through the motions of being committed to the Lord is deplorable. He peers through all of the pretense and sees the reality that lies beneath. Sadly, the hearts of the majority of the people of Israel were far from the Lord, yet they offered sacrifices and took part in festivals as if nothing was wrong. Our hearts should always delight in doing that which is pleasing in the sight of the Lord.

SUNDAY, Aug. 27.   Luke 18:9-14.
Humble faith. There can be a natural tendency for people to compare themselves with other people. This was the case for the Pharisee in Jesus' parable. In the Pharisee's estimation, he was superior to the sinful tax collector in every way. Under the guise of thanking God, he actually proceeded to exalt himself. The tax collector, however, is the one who exhibited humble faith and ended up being justified in the eyes of God.
—*Reginald Coats.*

PARAGRAPHS ON PLACES AND PEOPLE

PEREA

Although not mentioned by this name in the Bible, this region east of the Jordan River has a rich biblical history. The area, called Gilead, was given to the tribes of Reuben, Gad, and Manasseh as an inheritance (Josh. 22:9). It is believed to be the same region where the prophet Elijah was from (I Kgs. 17:1). In the time of Christ's ministry, it was part of the territory ruled by Herod Antipas, and it is where John the Baptist preached and baptized (John 1:28-29). When Jews were traveling between Jerusalem and Galilee, the preferred route passed through this area to avoid Samaria. Many of Jesus' teachings and miracles took place here, "beyond Jordan" (Matt. 4:15, 25; Mark 3:8; John 3:26; 10:40).

ABRAHAM'S BOSOM

This place of comfort and blessing is spoken of by Jesus in the story of Lazarus and the rich man (Luke 16:22-23). Jewish apocryphal writings describe "Abraham's bosom" as a place of blessing in *Sheol* for those who are awaiting the final judgment. Those who were wicked, like the rich man, would be sent to Gehenna—a place of torment in *Sheol*—to await final judgment. The image Jesus painted may reflect the Jewish custom of reclining to eat with the most favored guest positioned next to the host, leaning on his bosom (cf. John 13:23). "Abraham's bosom" is also considered by many to be an alternative term for heaven, where the righteous ones of God await their resurrection.

THE MULTITUDES

In a general sense, the multitudes referred to in the Gospels were the crowds that followed Jesus (Matt. 4:25; Mark 5:24; Luke 12:1). Translated from the Greek word *ochlos,* "multitude" is found primarily in the Gospel accounts. When used, it was usually describing a gathering of the common people that did not have a specific leader (Matt. 9:36). The multitudes were amazed at Jesus' teaching and miracles (Matt. 9:8, 33; Mark 11:18; Luke 13:17). Jesus is recorded as having compassion for the multitudes (Matt. 15:32; Mark 8:2). This is in contrast to the religious leaders, who had disdain for the multitudes (cf. John 7:31, 32, 40-49). The multitudes were easily swayed to turn on Jesus at His trial, calling for His crucifixion (Matt. 27:20-25; Mark 15:11-13).

THE TWELVE

Jesus called twelve men to be His closest disciples (Mark 3:14-19). The number twelve matches the number of the twelve tribes of Israel and looks forward to the twelve foundations of the New Jerusalem (Rev. 21:14). These men were with Jesus day in and day out during His three-year ministry. They learned His ways and the ways of God's kingdom. Jesus ordained them and sent them out (Greek: *apostellō*) to preach, heal, and deliver the people of Israel in His name. Later this mission was expanded beyond Israel to include all people (Matt. 28:18-20). The names of all twelve men are given in three places: Matthew 10:2-4, Mark 3:16-19, and Luke 6:14-16. The Twelve are: Simon (Peter) and his brother Andrew, James and his brother John, Philip, Thomas, Bartholomew (Nathanael), Matthew (Levi), James (son of Alpheus), Thaddaeus (Judas the brother of James), Simon (the zealot), and Judas Iscariot. After Christ's ascension, Matthias was chosen to replace Judas Iscariot (Acts 1:13-26).

—*Kelly Hawver.*

FOR COMFORT AND CHALLENGE

Plea at Evening
Beth M. Applegate

I've been so busy all day long!
Give me a moment. Let me pause to see
The beauty God created here—
The loveliness of earth and sky; the majesty
Of softly rounded, greening hill;
The sweep of clouds across the blue.
Bide for a moment. Let me be
So that I may feel and hear anew

Small birds that chant their evening song,
The little winds that shake and thrill
The branches of the elm trees.
Oh, let me contemplate the wondrous still
Of Him who gave such miracles to us,
Who speaks to me in still, small voice.
Wait! I'll be back to do the dishes.
Now let my soul rejoice.

When Heart Has Charity
Roy Z. Kemp

Who feasts alone at lavish board
And eats with selfishness
Shall find himself a starving soul,
His food a pottage mess.

But he who eats of scanty fare
But shares his piece of bread
Shall find his hunger well appeased
And see another fed.

The Sorry Sadducees
Edna Hirons

The Sadducees were sorry folk
Because of their belief,
And when they lost someone in death,
They must have felt deep grief,
For they did not believe as we
Who know of second birth.
They thought that life must end for one
When he passed from this earth.
How glorious it is to know
Of Jesus Christ, our King,
And know that life need never end
But is everlasting!

A Teacher's Prayer
Mary Mason

Oh, how I love the children;
Their innocence beguiles—
Appealingly enchanting,
Small faces wreathed in smiles.
With fresh-starched Sunday sweetness,

Small Bibles on display,
They join in "Jesus Loves Me,"
And then they bow to pray.

Somehow my heart is sobbing;
My soul is on its knees.
Please help me, Lord, as teacher,
To minister to these.